Photo Below: Sal with her Channel
support crew in Dover Marina, England

Photo Opposite: Sal with 10 year old
Ocean Brown in Jersey, Channel Islands

Foreword

"For me, the sea in its glorious natural state is where I find solace and peace. It is my natural habitat and always will be"

As I sit at home in Jersey relaxing and reflecting on my latest achievement – swimming the Channel from England to France and back to England again in 36 hours 26 minutes – I realise that this success has been a culmination of no less than 50 years of glorious sea swimming on both sides of the Atlantic - see my story in this book: Sal's Long Day Out.

I learned to swim properly aged 3-4 in the sea, as many others did. My first sea competition, which I won, was a 110 yards handicap race at Havre des Pas Bathing Pool (now known as The Lido). This is where it all began for me. I was 10 years old and we had no indoor pools in Jersey until I was 12, so we all started in the sea. Many local regular sea swimmers, like myself, hate pool swimming!

Over the years I have watched swimwear trends change dramatically. For me and many others who sea swim 'au natural', the choice is to simply swim in a swimsuit, cap and goggles.

I started wearing Happy Swimming and Happy Wild Swimming caps about 2 years ago and I love them! They depict my happiness in the sea 'to a T'.

I have shared this 'sea happiness' with many and I am so looking forward to this book ... as well as being happy swimming for many years to come.

Enjoy "Swimming with smiles"

Sal Minty-Gravett MBE

Contents

What's with all the smiles?

A smile is a wonderful thing. Times spent with family and friends, strangers or alone are always nicer when they're happy. Doing things which make other people smile makes us feel good too. So when we took an interest in learning how to swim outdoors a few years ago, a hobby some relate to as 'wild swimming', we found a new way to be happy. Others saw what we were doing and asked to join in.

We were swimming just off shore, along a coastline where various yachts, sightseeing ferries, jet-skiers and kayakers were passing by. It seemed wise to be visible in the water, so we looked to wear something bright.

Having constantly stated that we were *'happy'* while we were *'wild swimming'* we chose that as our name, along with a happy face design, on a bright orange swimming cap. Before we knew it, others were asking for them, so we set up a Facebook page to make it easy for anyone, anywhere in the world, to buy a cap and upload images of them being worn swimming or in fun poses. A choice of different cap colours and hoodies soon followed, optional wording of 'Happy Swimming' mainly for pool swimmers and this year, after a request from coldwater swimmers, the additional choice of wording 'Happy Cold Swimming'.

Swimmers like to say that they are happy swimming, so wearing a bright smile on your head keeps you safe, adds to your fun and will often put a smile on the faces of any onlookers too!

"Whatever your ability or personal reason for having a swim, always smile as you swim - you'll get out glad that you got in"

Photo by Simon John Parkin

Anyone can grab a 'happy cap' and join in the fun at Facebook group: Happy Wild Swimming

"Swimming with smiles" is a compilation of members own true stories told in their words and photographs to share their experiences, locations, special moments, recollections and happy feelings about swimming. We hope you enjoy them.

Gary & Claire

Founders of Happy Wild Swimming

Authors of "Swimming with smiles"

WEBSITES:

www.swimmingwithsmiles.com
www.happywildswimming.com
www.happyswimming.co.uk
www.altern8ives.com

The Happy Caps World Map

Swimming Is About People

Mark Johansen

Throughout my life, swimming whether wild or otherwise has made me very happy.

From those first strokes of doggy paddle to the last stroke of a marathon, swimming has always had the capacity to lift me. Maybe it's cups of tea in the club house after a cold winter swim, or the hearty breakfasts by the lake? Whether it's an easy swim with no particular aim, or the full on adrenaline rush of a race, who knows?

I can be alone with my thoughts, or swimming with friends, take comfort from the solitude or rejoice in the company and laughter. Swimming always makes me smile.

Swimming has kept me fit, it's given me a reason to get up in the morning and kept me going through the hard times. It helps me focus and put things in to perspective. It's my meditation, my relaxation and provides an outlet for frustrations and anxieties.

Swimming has helped me develop as a human being. You learn a lot about yourself on a long swim. As the hours tick by you visit dark places but coming through the other side changes you.

I've always thought it important to smell the roses along the way and open water allows this by putting me at one with nature. I love seeing the fish, the brush of weed against my skin, the waterfowl around me on the surface. The sting of cold water that quickly turns to the feeling of heat makes me marvel at how the human body functions in adverse

temperatures. The euphoria and happiness following a cold swim is indescribable - above all, swimming is about the people, the community.

These are people that give their time freely to help others. There's no edge to them, no one is out to break records. Instead, mutual respect, love and a genuine desire to see others succeed runs through their veins.

They've got the biggest appetites, but they've the hearts to match. Society as a whole could learn from their example.

Being a part of this slightly eccentric family is a gift, it's like being on a ride that you never want to end. The next swim could be half an hour or half a day long, but I know for sure it will be different than the last, it will be fun and it will be packed with amazing characters.

That makes me happy!

Sharing The Same Passion

Barry Hall

This is how I became a keen open water swimmer. It's 'my story'.

It all really began when we moved to the 'seaside'. It was 1961 and I was an eleven year old who couldn't actually swim! After several long hot summers when as kids we 'lived' on the beach every weekend, I was soon enjoying all that my new ocean playground had to offer ... and so began my love affair with the ocean.

I don't actually remember learning to swim. It just sort of happened as a result of playing in the sea every weekend. As the years went by I just loved spending my leisure time in, on, or under the sea. Scuba diving, water-skiing and windsurfing all gave me countless hours of pleasure and fun. During those years, I also learned how powerful and uncompromising the ocean can be and the importance of safety, even for the most experienced people. I was taught to respect the sea and never take it for granted. Otherwise, it would be certain to catch you out!

So now, in my more senior years, open water swimming has become my passion. A way of me keeping fit, meeting new friends and staying in touch with the sea.

I started by popping down to my local beach, Thorpe Bay near Southend-on-Sea, as an alternative to the congested 'chlorinated stew' that was my local pool. It was there that I first bumped into my friend, Penny, who was sitting outside her beach hut enjoying the afternoon sunshine. We started to chat and I discovered she was one of a group who were regular 'all year round' swimmers. I was invited to join in for some casual swims and soon became a regular with the group. All were very encouraging and supportive to newbies.

There was a real variety of abilities, from English Channel swimmers to casual dippers; everyone was very friendly and welcoming. So a swim followed by hot drinks (courtesy of Penny) and cakes, became a regular afternoon treat. I was soon going in 2-3 times a week for a 2km swim. It was a natural progression to go 'all year round' and I was rather overwhelmed by some of my hardcore friends who swam in skins with temperatures dipping under 5 degrees! But for me, (leading the wetsuit brigade), in a suit I could still enjoy the pain and exhilaration of swimming ... even with snow on the beach!

As time moved on, holidays were being planned with possible swim venues identified and meeting up with other local swimmers was invaluable in finding the best and safest areas to explore. It was during one such trip to Devon, that quite by chance I glanced up to spot in the

sea, a couple of 'happy caps'. I hastily scrambled into my wetsuit, cap and goggles then entered the water to race after the other caps. I caught up with the swimmers as they were resting mid-swim underneath Paignton Pier. It was then that I met Gary and Claire, who until then were just names on Facebook, known for running the group: Happy Wild Swimming

It was a welcome surprise to meet those who had created the very cap I was wearing. They decided to see safely ashore the swimmer they had been helping to become more sea confident and then joined me for a lovely swim back to Preston Sands.  Their friendship to folks like me and enthusiasm for open water swimming has undoubtedly been a major factor in the success of swimmers wearing their 'happy caps'. These are very popular right across the globe. Now, when passers-by look at the swimmers going in at Thorpe Bay, they can clearly see how many of us have joined the 'happy caps' phenomenon, as a variety of colours are on display!

During my holiday swimming trips, I have also sampled river and lake swims. I loved the vast expanses of water found in Cumbria, where my challenge has been to dip in every one of those great lakes.

Additionally, it was simply magical on regular trips to Norfolk and Suffolk, to experience the tranquillity of drifting along the rivers in 'Constable Country', accompanied only by the occasional kingfisher and waterfowl making their homes in this aquatic paradise.

So, what has open water swimming brought into my life?

First and foremost, it's been a great way to meet lots of new friends who share the same passion for 'wild swimming'. I have been very fortunate to have enjoyed their great friendship and hospitality over the past years.

Personally, I love the constantly changing moods of the sea. I somehow feel really alive when I can be part of the ocean. It is profoundly relaxing, a great way to stay in shape and I feel really privileged to have gained so much experience and pleasure from the wonderful environment that is the sea.

I'm definitely a very HAPPY WILD SWIMMER!

The Worldwide Weir

Karen Weir

I first caught the bug for open water swimming back in 2010 thanks to my brother, Andrew. Back then it was difficult to find like-minded people to join in with and none of my friends fancied it, nonetheless I was hooked!

In 2011, via Facebook, the Wild West Swimmers came to be and I joined them a few weeks after they formed. From the early days of dipping in Loch Lomond I have gone on to swim in many beautiful locations. Loch Lomond is my local, though the Lochs in and around the Trossachs are easily accessible to me, as is the Lake District.

I always swam year round with some of the Wild Westers, but in the early years I kept the wetsuit on only taking it off for a brief dunk at the end. Now it is a very different story, the wetsuit was ditched and I have gone on to take part in many Winter Swimming events in the UK and Worldwide. Slovenia, Estonia, Latvia and Argentina have been host to some of the events I have participated in and there are many more to choose from.

In 2015, I was offered the opportunity of a lifetime. I was invited by Matias Ola and the International Winter Swimming Association to represent Scotland in an event in Argentina.

Photo: Baltic Sea Estonia

The event comprised of two parts, first an International Relay Team swim across the Rio De La Plata from Uruguay back to Buenos Aires. The team was made up from swimmers from 21 countries and I was honoured to have been included in the selection. The team made history by swimming across the Rio De La Plata, rather than the approximate 45km predicted, due to poor conditions the distance covered was closer to 60km.

The second part of the Winter Swimming Festival took part in front of the iconic Perito Moreno Glacier (photo above). This was a winter swimming "gala" where I competed in many races in water of approx. 4/5 degrees. A stunning location and the memories of this will last a lifetime.

The Winter Swimming events are great fun; you meet many warm friendly people in the not so warm waters. In fact, through Facebook you can probably find people to swim with anytime, anywhere. I love nothing more than showing visiting swimmers the delights of swimming here in Scotland and some of those visitors included some fellow happy cappers!

Swimming is not all serious. It is good to mix it up with handstands, conga lines, underwater photography and general larking around as some of my pictures show.

Above: Happy Wild Swimming Caps conga in Loch Lomond

Below: Visiting swimmers receive a warm welcome all year round

Escaping To The Sea

Jodi Songhurst

As for lots of us my story really is about being 'happy'. I've always swum. My mum was a competitive swimmer (in her day a very good one!). She taught me whilst I was young and I too went into competitive swimming, until I became a typical lazy teenager and preferred 'vegging' in front of the TV!

Over the years, I returned to swimming often. Mainly as the most enjoyable way to keep fit, but, it was never quite good enough. Battling for space in a hot, sweaty, chlorine-drenched pool, upsetting slower swimmers, having to talk to people and having to follow the rules (both, the written and unwritten ones) of swimming and social etiquette.

Then, three years ago, a few friends suggested I try lake swimming. Reluctantly, rubber-clad, I did. Wow! There was space, scenery, weed, trees, mudfish, icy-cold water that froze my face and tasted 'brackish' at the nicest description. I was instantly addicted!

Until one day when we got to the lake to see our circuit cut to a smaller route to facilitate student party frolics on the lake. Angry, I almost didn't swim. In protest I got in without wearing my wetsuit. No one did that at this lake. Revelation! For me, the icy water on my skin is cathartic. The whole experience left me blissfully de-stressed and feeling incredibly alive (if a little hypothermic).

A short while after this, another friend persuaded me to join Beyond the Blue - a local sea swimming group full of an incredibly eclectic mix of people, who all love swimming in the sea. The lake became a distant memory. Why pay to swim in a lake when I have the gorgeous beaches of Poole just a few minutes drive away?

Now, I swim at least twice a week, all year round, in just my swimsuit, in all weather and all sea states. I know a lot of people ask 'why?' For me, it really is a lifeline. My home is about as hectic as they come. Two teenage daughters, one of whom is tipped to make the Tokyo Olympics GB Team for trampolining and went to Rio with the 'Olympic Ambition Programme' (designed for young athletes selected for their Olympic potential). I also have an 18 year old severely autistic son, Charlie, who, when happy, stands on our front wall jumping up and down waving a coat hanger at passing cars. When agitated, can become very violent and uncontrollable – my life is fun!

That may sound flippant, but in fact, my life is fun. When happy, Charlie is the most adorable 6'2" child ever. Everyone locally knows him and waves to him on our wall. You haven't lived until you've laid on the floor in a Tesco store aisle and 'swum backwards' along it, observing the fluorescent lighting strips with a fully-grown, good-looking Charlie by your side!

So, yes of course, the sea has become my escape. When my house is chock-full of teenagers, carers and other 'well meaning' people, I can't quite cope with, I escape. The sea always welcomes me, day or night. Sometimes with total serenity, other times with Nature's chaos. Occasionally, I swim on my own, though a lot of the time I meet other BTB-ers down there. Either way, once in the sea, head down swimming, it's just me and the cold water. Oh ... and the odd jelly fish!

Since starting my love affair with the sea, I've managed to drag my mum aged 72 years old, into it with me and we regularly swim together. She's still got it in the water. Although, we have to watch over her getting in and out when it's rough!

My partner, Tony, swims too, but not as much as I do. He joins me whenever he can. It's precious time spent together.

So there is the swim ... the sea ... and then, there are the people!

Open water swimming really does invite everyone into its arms. I have made so many new friends of all ages, sexes, backgrounds and sizes, it's phenomenal. It sure has broadened my horizons.

I've been swimming with Gary, Claire and other Happy Wild Swimming swimmers in Devon. I've swum in Liverpool docks, the length of Coniston and recently, to France as part of the 'Missed the Ferry' Channel relay team. I've also swum around Brownsea Island in Poole harbour.

My favourite swim has to be Durdle Door. It never gets old swimming under the Door. I think my first time was when I was 7 years old, with my mum. My most recent 'Door swim', at 45 years old ... with my mum!

What does Happy Wild Swimming mean to me?

It's simple. It's all about the sea and the company!

Photos: Top, at Burgh Island. Left, at Durdle Door

Jodi Songhurst with barrel jellyfish in Torbay, Devon
Photo: Claire Bunker-Fellingham

My Happy Place Is In Water

Susan Kirk

All swims are happy swims for me! For the past 20 years or so, whenever I was entered in an open water swim with body marking, my personal 'trademark' was for the body markers to include a smiley face on my arms, either inside my number (like in an 8, 9, 6, or 3) or just underneath it.

It was remarkable how contagious and soothing the smiles were amongst my fellow swimmers and the volunteers; a positive effect that I enjoyed sharing with others, inspiring them to smile and laugh as well.

I have also used my own inner 'swimming with a smile' strength to persevere through tough swims and to soothe my soul when faced with wild swims that were cut short by the uncontrollable elements.

The science says that the act of smiling releases endorphins and serotonin - two powerful neurotransmitters that contribute to pain relief and feeling good. I not only believe it, I also regularly practice swimming with a smile ... a big smile!

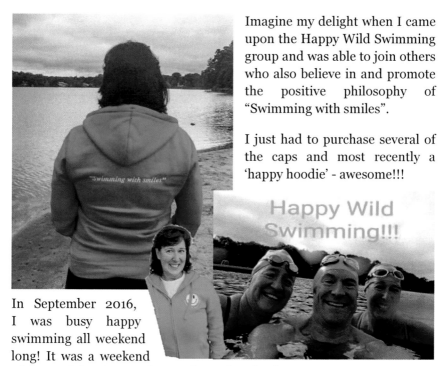

Imagine my delight when I came upon the Happy Wild Swimming group and was able to join others who also believe in and promote the positive philosophy of "Swimming with smiles".

I just had to purchase several of the caps and most recently a 'happy hoodie' - awesome!!!

In September 2016, I was busy happy swimming all weekend long! It was a weekend of memorial swims at the northern tip of Lake Hopatcong, New Jersey. On Saturday I completed the 9.11 Mile Memorial Swim and on the Sunday 2 mile, 1 mile and 1/2 mile swims. During our 9.11 mile swim, we had some very strong headwinds to deal with and boat traffic wakes which created a real washing machine effect out in the lake. My good swim buddy and relay mate said to me afterwards that she was channeling me and my joy of the bouncy conditions to help her get through her swim. I loved hearing that!

In preparation for another swim with the 'Jersey Girls', I ordered quite a few extra Happy Wild Swimming caps on my last order. I gave two of those caps to my Lake George Marathon Swim relay mates as a surprise and inspiration to help us get through the intended 18+ hours of Happy Wild Swimming. It is a 32 mile swim commemorating the first person to swim the length in 1958, Diane Struble. Since then, only 6 other solo swimmers and 1 relay team have successfully swum it. For the 2016 event only 14 individual swimmers and 14 relay teams were permitted.

I loved swimming in the beautiful bounce of Lake George, a long narrow lake located at the southeast base of the Adirondack Mountains in the state of New York. The 'Jersey Girls' and our stellar crew were totally prepared for the sustained headwinds that Mother Nature unleashed on us and enjoyed 4 bouncy, fun hours in the lake before it was called off for safety reasons due to the deteriorating weather conditions.

I am so proud of our entire team. Not only for our preparedness but also our execution, appreciation and the acceptance that Mother Nature always rules! Our entire team and crew are already planning a redemption swim in 2017.

My happy place is swimming in water ... any kind of water ... and I am thrilled to be able to share swimming smiles with all those that I meet along my swimming adventures.

The magic and allure of open water swimming events began for me at the beautiful Jersey Shore with the challenge of the accompanying surf!

I have enjoyed the deep blue seas of Hawaii during a relay swim across the Maui Channel and the gorgeous turquoise seas of Barbados

In the lakes of Las Vegas Nevada, Phoenix Arizona and Buttermere UK

With the Hudson River being a definite favourite spot; jumping off boats, swimming under iconic bridges and next to really big ships

... keep smiling and swimming!

Extra Swimming & Extra Smiles

Claire Bunker-Fellingham

From a young age I was encouraged to give everything a try, whether it was jumping in puddles, clambering around in woods, walking for miles in many different places or spending hours playing on the beach. I've always enjoyed being active, going out and about 'doing things' yet I've only delved into the world of swimming outdoors in recent years.

I've always loved swimming and was fortunate at primary school to have a fantastic swimming teacher called Mrs McClean. The small school pool wasn't the most inviting of environments, housed in a glass and corrugated plastic structure which rattled in bad weather, with changing rooms that were chilly and water in the pool that looked quite dubious at times! Yet despite all that I enjoyed learning to swim. She certainly had a knack of making me want to be there, challenging me to see if I could go that little bit further each time – "how about another length ... and then try another" I would hear from poolside. She taught me to feel confident in the water and for that I'll always be grateful. The swimming badges earned charted my progress and at the time enticed me to push the boundaries each time there was a chance to.

One of my proudest memories of those early swimming days is gaining my International STA 3km Long Distance Award when I was just 7 years old. Organised through my Brownies group we attended the local outdoor pool one Saturday morning to work towards our swimming badges. Each of us were assigned a spotter to monitor distance completed, ticking off each successful length. We had set our own targets as to what distance we wanted to achieve (mine was 1500m), but were also told that as long as we didn't stop we could ask the person monitoring how many lengths were needed to gain the next distance badge.

It was a beautiful day and I achieved my initial target, then just kept swimming and swimming! Asking every now and then how many more lengths were needed to get to the next level and continuing to swim. Everyone else had finished their respective badge distance, many had packed up and gone home but the lady monitoring me just let me continue for as long as I wanted to. I now had the pool to myself. She was as intrigued, as my onlooking parents were, as to how far I would actually go – when would I stop? That turned out to be at 101 lengths, having swum 3km! I was absolutely exhausted and a tad disorientated for the final lengths, of which the last few were by all accounts swum by me almost diagonally in the pool. Afterwards, I realised I had swum double the intended distance and was chuffed to bits.

I joined the local swimming club, regularly training a few times a week and competed in galas for several years. During my teenage years, it dawned on me that it was taking the edge off my actual enjoyment of swimming, so I stopped competitive swimming. Then as an adult I used pool swimming as my 'switch off' time, ploughing up and down the lanes, often covering a fair distance each session but without clock watching and it worked for me. Career commitments sometimes got in the way but I swam in the pool, following the black lines whenever I could.

It was a move to be by the sea in Devon that opened my eyes to outdoor swimming. I loved walking the coastal paths and paddling ankle deep in the sea, yet didn't swim in it! It seemed criminal to be so close, in beautiful surroundings and ignore doing something I'd always enjoyed. Swimming in the sea would be like the icing on a cake – why wasn't I doing it? On holidays abroad I'd happily swim in the sea, yet only took the occasional dip in UK waters. Something needed to change.

The deciding factor was realising the colder water here put me off getting involved. Wearing a wetsuit would help solve that problem, so Gary and I blindly set about purchasing wetsuits. Turning up at a local watersports shop I said I wanted to swim in the sea in a wetsuit that would keep me warm. The young lad sold me a 5mm/4mm winter surfing wetsuit saying it'd be warm and fine to swim in. Not having had a chance to try it out, I entered a charity 1 mile sea swim the following week. Shortly after entering the water I realised yes, I was cosy, but I was floating along like a lilo! With way too much buoyancy from the surf-suit, legs kicking out of the water, restricted arm movement and bobbing along on the surface, what should have been an easy enough swim for me turned into a long drag. One of the safety kayakers asked me several times if I wanted a tow back to shore as he could see what I was contending with. I knew I had it in me to finish, so I persevered and completed the swim.

Lessons learnt after that day? Next time research properly before buying a wetsuit! My surf-suit has now been relegated to just being used on occasional bob-about swims or if I think I'm going to be bashed up on rocks swimming through caves. I looked into it further and bought a proper fitting tri wetsuit (smooth outer neoprene) which makes a huge difference to swim in and provides more freedom of movement. I do swim in 'skins' (just wearing a swimming costume) too but haven't built up my tolerance to stay in the water for as long, so I tend to opt more often than not to wear my wetsuit knowing I can stay in a couple of hours or more and not be time restricted when we go off exploring as part of a swim. Each to their own, whatever you choose to wear as long as you are happy swimming, that's what counts.

There is something very special about swimming outside in the wild, be it sea, rivers or lakes. The freedom of space, fresh air, nature, opportunities to explore and seeing things from a whole different perspective are things I treasure. Despite being an avid pool swimmer for many years, since I started swimming all year round outdoors, I have only been back in an indoor pool once during the last 3 years.

The lure of 'Happy Wild Swimming' has caught me in its net!

Mindful of the things that put me off in the past, these days I enjoy the moments. I focus on the now. I still get my head down and swim but also remember to stop from time to time to appreciate the surroundings. The distance covered and what I've seen varies each swim. My longest sea swim to date has been 8km which was nice to do and I know I can still get on with covering a distance if I need to, but equally I've enjoyed many shorter fun swims with friends exploring different places, stopping to take time out to see and appreciate what's happening around us - like swimming to a natural arch. (photo above)

Sharing those swimming smiles with fellow swimmers and onlookers too feels great. On another one of our swims around a headland, a group of us all wearing our 'happy caps' came around the corner and started swimming alongside the beach hut lined promenade towards the beach. We heard a voice on the prom singing out loud and beckoning us over towards him. As we got closer it was apparent that the elderly gentleman, out for a stroll with his wife, was serenading us with his rendition of "When you're smiling ... the whole world smiles with you". He was beaming and called out to tell us that seeing all the happy faces as we swam past in the water had made their day. He thanked us for sharing that moment of happiness. Extra smiles all round that day!

Crazy Cold Desire

Barry O'Connor

The sea and swimming to me is a constant. It's something that has always been in my life. I could swim before I could walk. I am lucky to live in Dublin and have easy access to the water. I miss it when I am not near it.

I do the majority of my swimming in and around the South Dublin coastal area, specifically The Forty Foot near Dun Laoghaire. It is a fantastic location as it can soothe your soul or challenge you depending on your needs. We have a small club called 'The 40 Foot Walruses Winter Swimmers' which has travelled to some interesting places.

The crazy desire to test ourselves in cold water has taken us to various locations including:

St. Petersburg, Russia; Jelgavas, Latvia; Reykjavik, Iceland; Gdansk, Poland; Murmansk and Tyumen, Russia, as well as Lake Windermere, UK

I am fortunate to have two travelling companions, Ger Kennedy and Allen Evans.

Both are very supportive and just on the edge enough, to ensure that our trips are always good fun!

To most people it may seem to be odd that we can talk about having fun in water at -0.9C, but somehow we do. We manage to try to have some fun in most of the things we do, while at the same time we recognise the safety net provided by the likes of the RNLI and other voluntary services.

I love being part of the Facebook group, Happy Wild Swimming. There are some truly awesome swimmers, who have achieved incredible things and there are people who are discovering the joys of swimming when, most people say you shouldn't until the summer. I love the fact that all the photos are of people smiling while having fun in their own way and just enjoying it. I think the map of the locations is very cool and I am proud to have contributed in a very small way to this. Please, keep it up!

I Have My Illness To Thank

Debbie Pentland

Hi, I am Debbie, 57 years old and I live in Southsea on the South Coast of England. Although I am from Edinburgh, Scotland, I like the English weather far more, especially for wild swimming!

I only learned to swim properly a couple of years ago after I was diagnosed with a third autoimmune disease. I have Systemic Lupus Erythematosus, Raynaud's and Lambert-Eaton Myasthenic Syndrome. There is no cure for any of them. However, I have managed to come off all medication by using exercise and healthy eating. Well, most of the time, as you all know, us swimmers need our cake! In a way I have my illness to thank for me getting into all this sport.

I was diagnosed with Lupus and Raynaud's when I was 32. I was told I would have to be on medication for the rest of my life and I would have to

'modify my lifestyle' as these diseases were very debilitating with one of the main symptoms being extreme fatigue. This was like 'a red rag to a bull' for me to be told what I could and could not do.

My wonderful husband Bob told the rheumatologist "you don't know who you're dealing with here." Anyway after six years on a cocktail of drugs and spending that time improving my fitness and nutrition I was able to come off all my medication. I stayed drug free for sixteen years.

In October 2011, I took part in the Beachy Head Marathon and my legs just went from under me. For several months I had not felt right but just thought my Lupus was trying to show me who was boss. A few days later I was rushed into hospital wheeled in a chair, as I could not use my legs, I could not lift my arms up, I was slurring my speech, having trouble swallowing and I had double vision. I was terrified. My rheumatologist did a few tests and told me he suspected that I had yet another autoimmune disease but I had to be moved to the Neurological Hospital Southampton. I spent six of the most frightening weeks of my life in hospital where I was told I would be on disability as I would not work again. I was also told I would be on medication for life and I would need to have a stair lift fitted in my house as I would not manage the stairs.

Well, that was 2011. I spent two years getting fitter, making more changes to my nutrition, taking a few swimming lessons and joining the Portsmouth Triathletes. After two years I was once more able to come off all medication and have been drug free for over two years now. My neurologist was amazed and quite frankly, so was I!

I have always had a positive attitude to life and a sense of fun. I truly believe this has helped me achieve all that I have done.

If you would like to read my story in more detail I have self-published a book on Amazon 'Mutiny In My Body' and all my share of the sales go to Lupus and Myasthenia charities.

With Raynaud's I cannot wild water swim all year around but I make the most of every opportunity during the months of May-October.

Happy Wild Swimming my friends!

Beauty And The Bathing Pools

Ciprian Ilie

I've never had any formal swimming training, no school swim lessons (there wasn't a single pool in my childhood town), so I grew up fairly scared of water. Especially coming from a generation, where they'd just throw you in and hope for the best and find your crying highly amusing. I think I was about 13 years old when I 'learnt to swim'. That is to say, I mastered moving all my limbs in such a manner I would manage not to drown until I got to safety. The setting was a fast flowing, muddy river in the countryside.

Born and raised in Romania, I was lucky to marry a Guernsey girl and I now live on a beautiful island in the middle of the English Channel. Guernsey may be British, but it is situated far closer to the French coast - so much so, you can see France with the naked eye.

I really enjoy the fun side of swimming in one of the many beautiful bays on the islands, more often than not with my doggies, all of whom absolutely love the water!

Maybe that was why I was attracted to the Happy Wild Swimming caps with their emphasis on fun adventure and exploration of our beautiful coast and natural surroundings.

My ambition is to one day cross the English Channel ... on a ferry, with a big car I could fill with French wines and cheeses. Joking aside, the Channel Islands are a breeding ground for great swimmers, but my love of the sea and all things swimming is relatively new.

A few years ago I set myself the challenge to swim all year round, inspired by the many hardy and mixed bunch of folks I would see by the Bathing Pools. The pools get filled directly from the sea at high tide. The height of the walls allows a certain amount of water to remain in the pool as the tide lowers. The walls also stop an excess of seaweed or sea creatures finding their way into the pools. This makes it the perfect venue for winter swimming as you are outside in the elements, in the sea, but safe. Guernsey people have been lucky to enjoy these facilities since 1865.

In its earlier years, the pools were often visited by many people of great significance, including legendary 'Les Misérables' writer Victor Hugo and famous Renaissance painter Pierre-Auguste Renoir.

Lake Swimming Around Europe

Alistair Mackintosh

Henleaze Lake – Bristol, England

My first introduction to lake swimming was about ten years ago when I discovered, thanks to my wife, that we lived five minutes' walk away from the most beautiful, tranquil swimming lake in the area – bizarrely right in the middle of suburban Bristol. I joined her on the waiting list and within a short time we were members and swimming regularly.

Since joining the lake, we have been swimming every year for ten years during the swim season (May - September). Even having two children in the meantime hasn't stopped us, though it does mean we now need to take it in turns to pop down, instead of swimming together. Living so close by makes it infinitely easier to squeeze in a quick swim between other responsibilities and is surely the best way of unplugging from a hard day at work, plunging in and washing away the cares of the moment.

The lake itself has developed too since we joined – the swimming area has extended to make a good 250 metres circuit and there are regular events too – a long swim (during which they close off the fishing area at the far end and

allow everyone to swim right the way down), early swims on a Friday morning (during which breakfast is often available) and there is now even a sauna too – very popular. Along with the sauna, they have also introduced Winter Swimming – a great way

to make use of my 'Happy Cold Swimming' cap. I have been partaking in the winter swimming this season – I use a wetsuit to keep the asthma at bay and it also means I don't need to spend immense amounts of time warming up in the sauna afterwards. Of course, the only time winter swimming is not allowed is when the lake is iced over!

One of the highlights of the summer is that my eldest daughter qualified for membership having completed her 50 metres swimming test in the lake to prove her eligibility. A new generation of Happy Wild Swimmers has begun and hopefully my youngest daughter will also qualify in the next year or two meaning we can all go down together.

Llyn Geirionydd – Snowdonia, North Wales

Martina, my wife, grew up in North Wales and as we both work in education, we are able to make good use of the holidays by going up there to stay pretty regularly. There are many good spots to do wild swimming in the Snowdonia area, though you do need to be careful as some lakes are used for reservoirs and some are even rumoured to be full of lead - always good to check first if you are not sure! One of my favourite Lakes around there is Geirionydd, which is not far from the tourist spot of Betws-y-Coed. You can drive to the lake directly but it is much nicer to drive to Lake Crafnant and take an hour or so to walk over the hill and appreciate the views and the forest along the way.

The lake itself is fine to swim in, though sometimes they have one end roped off for speedboats. If not, there are many places to get in and the lake has stunning scenery around, to appreciate whilst you are having a dip. As I am not swimming for fitness, I always like to swim breaststroke, which enables me to have a good look

around and take in the views at the same time as swimming.

This year I went for a swim with my brother in law, who is also starting to get the outdoor swimming bug.

It was a gorgeous day and the swim really enhanced what was already a great walk with our kids.

It definitely adds a new meaning to the phrase 'being at one with nature' when you are actually immersing yourself in it too!

Donauwoerth Lake – Bavaria, Germany

The third lake that we visit regularly is not in the UK but in Germany, about an hour north of Munich. We have friends, now living in a small town called Donauwoerth, who we met at our antenatal classes before our first daughter was born. We have kept in contact ever since. They kindly invite us to stay every year for a week and as well as having an excellent 'Freibad' (open air swimming pool with amazing slides), they also have a number of swimming lakes too. We have all had a swim in three or four of the different lakes and our favourite one is the closest to their house. It is open to the public at any time and they often have community events held there.

There is a great area for kids to swim in too, which is sectioned off with some logs and they can easily stand up if they are not so confident– a great introduction to wild swimming without any of the risks.

My most memorable swim there actually took place this year. We had a particularly warm day (up in the 30C's) followed by a much cooler and rainy day. I guessed that there wouldn't be many people swimming in the lake with the rain but the water should still be warm from the previous day. I was proved right and had the whole lake to myself as I swam from

one side to the other in a light drizzle. I found it slightly eerie but a magical experience.

Lake Kournas – Crete, Greece

The last lake I would like to describe is one that we only discovered in August 2016 and is arguably the most stunning. It is called Lake Kournas in the equally stunning Crete. The freshwater lake itself is very blue and surrounded by huge hills. The photos don't entirely do it justice about how impressive the setting is.

The water is very shallow for quite a while – again, perfect for introducing kids to the pastime of wild swimming. There were actual goldfish swimming around with us too, (introduced to the lake historically, rather than being native) and a couple of geese joined us for a while as well.

Once you are tired from swimming, you can take some time to tour round the wider lake in a pedalo, having a dip whenever you feel like it from the back of the boat, some of which even included slides.

Of course the ice creams and 'Freddo' cappuccinos are also a very enjoyable way of restoring the energy levels too!

Majestic Ice Crystals

Shaun Hales

Galdhopiggen is the highest mountain in Norway, Scandinavia at 2469 metres and has one of the few year-round ski slopes. Two weeks into our backpacking trip we had gravely underestimated the weight of our bags. Needless to say we were knackered, yet strangely spurred on to see more. The beauty of Norway was spellbinding and we couldn't stop. The second I saw it from the bus window, I gasped and I knew I had to do it. At the base of the peak the snow merged into an icy lake, glistening in the evening sun, a smile slowly spread across my dry chapped lips. The hike to the summit was tomorrow and I couldn't miss checking out the crevasses, so it was now or never. Tent pitched, kit left behind, we set off.

As we got closer the best sound in the world was coming from the water, ice chimes. Imagine a field of ice crystals gently chinkling each other in the breeze. I slowly got in and swam across the crystal maze to the middle where the ice had frozen into slabs. I only stayed in for a dip as it was a tricky path across the boulders back to any form of heat, plus we were exhausted from travelling.

It wasn't my longest or hardest swim but it was by far the most majestic!

Happy To Remember

Jane Bell

Very roughly my involvement with happy caps stems from the loss of my best friend and swimming partner, Tony Mellett. Those who know me will have heard this before, but in a nutshell, in the days following his death, Tony's wife Sarah, gave me his smiley face hat as a keepsake. I have worn it during all the swims that we had planned together.

Tony's side-kick, the 'other Tone' Tony Marshall, then introduced me to Happy Wild Swimming caps so I wear mine with reference to my friend.

I think lots of my Redcaps club friends wear their happy caps for the same reason. We had a memorial swim for him this year to mark the 2nd anniversary of his passing and I asked those attending to wear a smiley. The turnout was just fantastic!

Also, I'm known for wearing my smiley face swimming costume bought as a tribute to Tony, for the 1st anniversary of his death.

Right: Wearing my happy cap and smiley costume during a visit to Scotland

Sarah Mellett sent this message to Gary: "I have a happy cap too from Tony Marshall who was best friends with my late husband who sadly passed away 1st May 2014 of a totally unexpected massive heart attack. Jane is such a wonderful friend and has been extremely supportive. So you see the smiley or rather Happy Wild Swimming caps have a rather poignant meaning for me and a lot of friends in the club. Many thanks!"

When A Smiley Swam To France

Lorraine Rate

When Tony Marshall asked me a few years ago to coach him to attempt a solo crossing of the English Channel in 2015, I instantly knew that I had a serious challenge on my hands. Not from a training perspective, but because I knew I first needed to tap into his serious side. Was there even a serious side to him? All who know him will appreciate his larger than life character and his unique way of messing about, yet kind of training hard at the same time.

He brings out the best in people. He makes them laugh all the time.

So it wasn't any surprise to me that he hitched up with the Happy Wild Swimming caps team and started ordering dozens of happy swimming and happy wild swimming caps, plus happy dryrobes and even had his own smiley face design printed on the bottom of his swimming trunks.

It didn't matter how good or bad training was going, swimming behind a smiley bottom for endless lengths of the pool always made me chuckle.

When it came to the swim Tony insisted that we all wear our happy swimming caps for his little venture across the English Channel.

Left: happy washing line

Right Smiley trunks

49

He succeeded in his solo swim on a day when others didn't. He stuck with it relentlessly for an incredible 20 hours 12 minutes, despite seasickness, jellyfish and terrible weather conditions – he was smiling all the way!

At the half way point we played a music track from the boat with the chorus blurting out loud the lyrics, "We're halfway there!" His witty response was to ask, "How far have I swum?"

He finally landed on the beach in France in the dark, exhausted, with Jane Bell and I swimming in behind him as support. The three of us shared that wonderful moment of joy. These photos taken at the time show the emotion for all involved.

Then there was reflection, since the swim had been dedicated to the 'Other Tony' his best buddy and Jane's partner, who had passed away suddenly prior to Tony beginning his training with me.

It was a milestone for Tony and Jane, who took time to write their own personal dedication in the French sand, in memory of their missing friend.

Tony has now booked his two-way crossing attempt in 2017 and that can only mean one thing - lots and lots more smiles!

... and now I have even had a smiley face designed costume made just for me! I would enclose a picture of my bottom in my costume, but as Tony always used to say, EVERY TIME we swam together, "Does my bum look big in this?" I am now thinking, my bum definitely looks big in mine!

... but a 'double Smiley bottom' shot will no doubt follow!

Tony's swim successfully raised much needed funds to help bring more smiles to the children of Little Havens Hospice, a charity close to his heart.

A year later, in July 2016, Tony coached and swam with his own English Channel Relay Team to a successful one-way crossing.

The team members of Chalkwell Redcaps were all treated by Tony to their own individual happy dryrobes, along with Happy Wild Swimming caps. Each wore one for a section of their swim and his partner Louise also wore a Happy Cold Swimming cap to record the first Cold cap to swim to France!

See his story:

"Happy Channel Relay Team"

Saved By Strangers

Gary Standen

Shortly after I turned 9 years old, I found myself sitting on the floor of a swimming pool looking up at the surface, relying on the kindhearted assistance of a complete stranger.

We all have family or friends who've helped us at some point, yet often our lives are influenced by strangers who we do not get to thank.

It was to be an eventful fortnight during the summer school holidays.

I had yet to learn to swim. Keen to be 'part of the gang' I joined a bunch of local boys of similar and slightly older age to me to enjoy a nice sunny day at the Black Rock open air pools in Brighton. It was the place of fun. It included a small ankle deep paddling pool which I was accustomed to using and a traditional full length main pool with high diving platforms where the water was a huge 10 feet deep - none of which I went anywhere near. The whole complex was separated from the sea by a small retaining wall, which added a thrill for most people, though for me it was an additional fear, since I couldn't swim a single stroke.

That day the older boys laid out their towels around the main pool, so I did too. We all chatted for awhile, then some schoolboy 'messing about' took a sudden turn and I found myself being chased around the edge of the pool. A brief moment of pushing and shoving projected me into the water in the diving area, where I instantly sank to the bottom. The soles of my feet were resting on the pool floor before I even registered that I had been pushed. There I stayed for the next few minutes. It was quite surreal, calmly looking up at the ceiling of watery images, with swimmers feet dangling, sunshine glistening through the surface and a flurry of white splashes as another diver entered from the boards. As an adult I'm confident and I happily speak up when I need to. Yet as a well-mannered, shy, 9 year old boy, brought up in an era of 'speak when you're spoken to', there I was calmly being quiet on the bottom of the pool. Not making a fuss, nor raising my voice. In fact, I remember listening to numbed voices of others playing on the surface above as a trail of bubbles left my nose and mouth drifting up to join the splashing feet overhead. I believe I actually enjoyed that moment of solitude and visuals I'd never seen before. After all, I'd not drowned before, so it was interesting to see!

I cannot recall when the calm ceased or the nice views ended. The next thing I remember, I was spluttering poolside, laying on my side. A young male lifeguard and an older lady swimmer were crouched over me asking if I was alright. I think I mumbled, "Yes" before standing up to seek out my friends, all had returned to their towels poolside ignorant to my little adventure with near-death. In fact, embarrassed and not wishing to admit to my non-swimming standard, I never said a word and just laid-down to warm in the summer sunshine. That was the first of the strangers I have never been able to thank, but who influenced my life in a huge way. After all, I'm still alive.

I'd like to say that was my only brush with death, but a week later I was repeating my antics in a different pool. My parents had agreed to meet visiting relatives for a day at Saltdean Lido, a wonderful 'art deco' outdoor pool. One which Claire and I returned to enjoy as adults many years later. However, as the ill-fated 9 year old that day, I was in the water again. I had been instructed by my Dad to wear inflatable armbands and was happily letting them carry me as I kicked a doggy-paddle style of leg flicks. I drifted across the pool on my own, taking in all the fun being had by other swimmers and then I stopped kicking, allowing the armbands to support me. Minutes later, I felt my back resting up against the lane divider that stretched the width of the pool, dividing the deepest end from the rest of the pool. For some reason I chose to slip my arms behind me and up over the rope, trapping my armbands and effectively handcuffing me to the rope. Immediately my legs floated up behind me, placing my face in the water, like one of those ornamental dipping birds. The more I kicked the more my head stayed under. In contrast to my previous calm adventure, this time sheer panic set in. I frantically kicked harder and faster as I felt my chest tighten and saw a mass of bubbly water appear in front of me. Then, with a sudden squeak, my thin weedy arms slipped out of the armbands and down I plummeted. Once again I was heading for the pool floor. This time it was different. I wasn't enjoying it. I felt scared and there was no moment to reflect. Just a mass of thrashing in water and a crushing pain in my chest. I fought for breath for awhile, before I just went limp ... and then silence. Probably the briefest of moments, though one which frightened me enough to give me nightmares for years. During the silence I watched a delicate hand appear from the surface and fumble to grab my wrist. That's all I remember, a delicate hand fumbling. It went black after that – another stranger available at the right time!

I woke up (that's how it felt coming round) to see gushes of water leaving my mouth and nose, a lifeguard pushing on my chest and the woman who had yanked me out smiling a big smile. She wrapped me in her towel, giving me the biggest of hugs. I sat there drying out for a few minutes, before it dawned on me I was meant to be joining my family at the picnic they'd set out on the grass area, out of view behind a windshield barrier separating the picnic lawn from the pool. As a child in panic mode, I ditched her towel, grabbed my armbands and without a word ran off to join my family. It wasn't the happiest reunion after a second near-death experience, as my strict dad had been looking for me and so scolded the back of my legs for being late for lunch. I knew his burst of anger was actually his own panic, worried he'd lost me and his over protective nature came out in a frustrated slap. He hadn't heard me answer his question of "Where have you been?" with an embarrassed, "I've been drowning!" I was simply told to sit down and eat the lunch my Mum had prepared for us. I couldn't tell her what had happened either, she was a non-swimmer who, apart from achieving her school-enforced 10 yards certificate, was so scared of water she wouldn't walk near it let alone swim. So I chose not to tell her that I'd been pulled out twice in two weeks. Although, as I sat there munching on my jam sandwich, I vowed to either never go in again or learn to swim soon.

A short time after, I heard friends say they were taking swimming lessons one evening, so off my own back, I tagged along intending to watch them at the local St Luke's indoor pool. Two of them had been at my first drowning, though they were still unaware I couldn't swim a stroke, they thought I was joining to do intermediate lessons with them. So imagine their faces when, because I hadn't taken any costume, I appeared poolside with the retired male trainer wearing a pair of white Y-fronts, from the lost property box, tied at the waist by a length of brown string! Yes, that's what the trainer insisted I wear! Ever since, when I hear the expression 'How long is a piece of string?' I instantly recall how tight he tied my waist that night and reply, "Not long enough!"

He gave me no choice of going home to do it another week, shouting, "You're here, you're going in and you will swim tonight!" I never argued. Not even when the friends laughed harder than they had ever before at the sight of me in 'grandad underwear', hanging off a wooden pole being dragged along in the water for my first lesson. Nevertheless, that experienced trainer did get me in and by the end of that lesson I'd let go of the pole and splashed my first self-supporting doggy-paddle stroke. It wasn't pretty, it wasn't far, but it was me 'staying above the water' at last!

He was another stranger to thank, who I never saw again. My dad heard what I had achieved and arranged formal swimming lessons from the following week at the Brighton Swimming Club in what was the old North Road 'cold water filled' pool. You quickly learned that to stay warm you had to swim. By the age of 10 and twice the height of the 4 year olds learning with me, I finally swam my first width, then my first length, taught by Nina, the swimming club instructor who couldn't swim herself! Instead, she relied on a huge hook on a pole to retrieve troubled beginners. She was always bubbly and would give a big smile before firmly shoving us in, demanding "Swim! Just swim!" Despite never experiencing it herself, she guided me that first year towards swimming one length, gaining my first and only swimming medals of a bronze for breaststroke and silver in backstroke in a club gala. However, I gave up swimming soon after as I had started at a grammar school which didn't have a pool, the nearest public pool being two bus rides away. Also, as big a crime as it was living in a coastal town, instead of going to the beach at weekends, I preferred kicking a football (which is another story). I didn't swim much at all over the rest of my adult years. The odd holiday splash and a few attempts to join Claire in a pool when she would happily swim 100 lengths during an evening switch-off after work, while I'd rest more than swim.

It was our move to Torbay, Devon, which finally enticed me to embrace sea swimming, aged 52. It was the right time for me. It was our decision to make a lifestyle change of work-leisure balance on the back of Claire having 'saved my life' – not a stranger to thank this time, but the one closest to me. She had nagged me about getting some skin checked out and being a 'typical man' I delayed it three times before attending my doctor. Before I knew it, I was in hospital having the first of 11 operations over 6 years and being advised that I needed to tell my life insurance company I was now a cancer patient. I calmly accepted the news, just grateful I'd been nagged to get it sorted. Not being able to donate blood has been disappointing though, as Claire still gives as often as allowed.

Years later, halfway through my own treatments, I was exiting the sea and was questioned by a stranger as to why I was in a wetsuit on a warm day. I explained my reason for covering-up and he suddenly looked very concerned and asked if I'd check his shoulder. Sure enough it was a very dodgy mole, so I insisted he visit his GP that very afternoon. I explained we were moving along the coast the following week, but wished him well. I didn't know it but weeks later he had turned up on the beach near our new home for 3 days running on the off-chance of spotting me. When I eventually swam by he called out, meeting me at the shoreline with a tear in his eye and holding out his hand. He grasped my dripping wet hand very tightly and shaking it continually repeated, 'Thank you'. He had been sent to hospital that day and they operated a few days later. He said I had saved his life - a stranger was thanking me!

I've also been involved directly in some other 'saved by a stranger' events. Twice involving hypothermia striking non-regulars attending swims with friends, in recent years, local to where we now enjoy our own regular 'Wild' sea swimming. The first was before Happy Wild Swimming days when we joined another 'Wild Swimming' group to swim around a headland and a boyfriend of a swimmer had joined in wearing just his snorkel mask, flippers and shorts as it was a warm day. However, he was totally unprepared for how quickly he would get cold in the deeper water. His girlfriend and others were so busy having fun they all missed him go quiet and just float almost head-in. I swam over to check if he was just looking at fish, but his mask was steamed up and he didn't respond at first, so I suggested he flip on his back and use his flippers to get to shore. He gave me the thumbs up and started to kick away. Luckily, I kept my eye on him reaching shore, as while others got out to get changed, he remained laying on his back in the shallow surf, not getting out. I pulled him in and called for a swimmer who was a nurse to help. She had us all mass-hug him for gradual body warmth, then wrap him and feed him a drink. Half an hour later he was being told what had happened. The second was a similar situation, when an occasional swimmer in our newly formed group brought along a spear-fisherman friend to enjoy the sea caves just 50 metres along the coast. While he swam off taking photos, I saw the tell-tale signs from his friends' lips and eyes. I pulled him out, supported him to frog-march him the few hundred metres over the beach and into our nearby garden. I wrapped him in my dryrobe and Claire fetched him a warm drink, which he was halfway through before his eyes refocused fully and he asked where he was. The last he recalled was getting into the water! He was a healthy young policeman and a part-time fitness instructor. Yet he had fallen to hypothermia in a few minutes when his core temperature dropped quickly. Another lesson learned and another swimmer saved by a stranger. Although, he did get to thank me and accepted my lessons before joining us for several swims – safely!

There is a sting in the tail of this story though. Not everyone gets saved.

I had my young children visiting when I took a call from the police who couldn't get hold of a next of kin to identify a drowned man believed to be my ex-wife's younger brother and they asked me to tell her. A freak wave had snatched 20 people standing knee-high on a beach. All were rescued by the safety boat apart from the one pulled last from the water - my 6 foot 4 inches strongly built ex-brother-in-law. One of the hardest things I've ever done was to sit on the sofa with an arm around each young daughter and explain why they wouldn't see their favourite uncle again.

I wasn't a swimmer then and had taken my girls on holidays without any thought that freak waves occur. The RNLI volunteers and other lifesavers are wonderful - they save strangers and just carry on to the next call out.

Thanks to strangers who saved me, who I never got to thank (and to Claire who I'll thank forever), I've never again found myself sitting on the pool floor waiting for assistance. Often, I remember those times, keeping in mind the sea is always 'boss', as I plunge off rocks into waves or explore sea caves all year round as part of the Happy Wild Swimming group. I'm pleased to have given back by way of helping others, some complete strangers, to get in the water and learn to swim – no thank you required.

Where will I go?

Where have I been?

All that I've done

All that I've seen

A place to see

A place to feel

Time to reflect

Time to be still

Words: Gary Standen

Swimming With Style

Diego De Los Rios

First and foremost I'm a swimmer.

However, I got into taking pictures and making swimming videos as a recruiting tool. Ever since I moved to sunny Miami, Florida, USA, it's hard not to want to take a picture.

I would swim every morning from the beach at 12th Street Ocean Lifeguard Station.

Every time and every day, I would see something amazing. But those images would only stay with me, so I thought why not share them? Why not show others that the ocean is a happy place to swim? I started taking pictures of myself swimming, always wearing the same cap. I wanted to bring more energy to my pictures, so I decided to start collecting swimming caps and enjoyed always swimming with style.

Thanks to one of the other well known Facebook groups, I found out about the Happy Wild Swimming caps. I knew I had to have one as that wording was so suited - it was my mantra! What I was

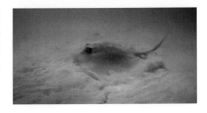

doing *every* morning. Only this time, I would be wearing it on my head and sharing the 'happy' smiley face with other swimmers ...

... and hopefully getting others to join in, enjoying the sea, like me.

Photos: Sea Swimming in Miami, Florida

I've enjoyed several swimming events in recent years one is the 'Swim For Alligator Lighthouse', a 9 mile race that takes place in Islamorada, Florida. Swimmers swim out in tropical open water about 4 miles to the lighthouse and back to shore, swimming through one of the largest reef systems in the Florida Keys. The venue is now really famous thanks to the Netflix show 'Bloodline' which was filmed right on the spot where the swim takes place. 2 years ago it was the first time I'd entered that race and the first time I'd swum that kind of distance. On that occasion, I

swam 4 miles without hydrating; only stopping to hydrate at the lighthouse itself. So on my way back my arms started cramping, making it a tough finish to the race, although I gained a very pleasing 3rd place.

Two years on, having learned from my previous experience, this year I returned to the same swim and it was smooth sailing. I hydrated every 30 minutes, felt good throughout the swim and achieved 2nd place.

I may not have won those races, but I have claimed a few firsts I am proud of. When I bought my happy cap I was told by Gary that I was the first swimmer in the USA to wear one.

In addition, I was the first member to upload a video clip into the group Happy Wild Swimming of a swimmer (me!) swimming whilst wearing a happy cap.

Note: Happy Wild Swimming in Spanish translates as Feliz Natacion Salvaje

Jed braving a cold dip at Pen Y Gwryd

Snowdonia National Park

Ever Seen A Smiley And Not Smiled?

Lucy Dunstan-Beasley

Borne of a love of certificates and badges, it was sheer bloody mindedness rather than any kind of aquatic aptitude that led me to learn a basic width of lifesaving doggy paddle at primary school and (because I wanted the badge) a determinedly laboured 25 metres of front crawl.

Lamentably, I didn't have the required co-ordination for breaststroke and still can't do more than a few metres without sinking slowly to the bottom. So it looks like I'll never get that elusive 25 metres breaststroke badge!

That was it for me and swimming for many, many years. Until, in 2013, a freak accident while skating left me unable to run, hop or jump. Miserable and sore, my doctor said, "Why don't you swim?" So I limped to my local chlorine pit and attempted to recreate the glorious ASA badge days of my youth. Sadly, it became apparent that I'd need lessons if I wanted to make it safely to the deep end. So I enrolled in an adult beginner's class in the baby pool, which to my delight, I enjoyed immensely. The baby pool was too hot and too shallow ... and I loved it!

Any swimmer will tell you that when it all joins together and you feel good, the feeling of the water moving over your body, the sound of it, the pressures you apply to the liquid to propel yourself on and through and past, all these things are meditative and you start to dream. 'Swish' ... this is amazing. 'Swoosh' ... I feel unstoppable. 'Swish' ... I wonder if this is how Channel swimmers feel? 'Swoosh' ... I reckon I could swim the Channel. 'Swish' ... I wonder how far it is? 'Swoosh' ... it can't be *that* far, right? So, buoyed by my graduation out of adult beginners' class in the baby pool, I signed up to swim the English Channel, blissfully ignorant of the dangers and the distance I had to travel.

In between times, there were months of training. So many people to thank for their encouragement, motivation and inspiration. I shamelessly drilled everyone I met for information, learned by getting it right, learned by getting it wrong and swam in all sorts of conditions. As a handy hint for Channel aspirants, if the Dover Beach Training crew tell you to get in and swim, don't counter with "But I'd never have to swim the Channel in this rain/sleet/fog/swell/murk". You'll find yourself with extra time added and a boot up the butt as you descend the pebbled beach to the sea.

This brings me finally, circuitously, to the purpose of this ramble - my Happy Wild Swimming cap.

Firstly, let's just get this out of the way. Training to swim the Channel isn't always happy. It is often sore and boring too.

My Channel swim was in September and early in the season I had been given a 2 hour swim.

I'd swum further and longer in the pool, so the distance wasn't a problem, but my mindset was. After an hour, I'd convinced myself I was too cold to go on. After an hour and a half, I tried to quit and get out. A veteran Channel swimmer calmly blocked me from exiting the sea, then jumped in and coaxed me into continuing. Coaching me through my final half hour and staying with me stroke for stroke.

Huddled on the beach sipping scalding coffee afterwards, my peers and mentors loving and supportive explained that endurance swimming is as much a mental game, as a physical one. "You must use your brain to keep you going. You must start and stay, positive."

I sat on the beach after my disastrous swim, embarrassed that I had to be thrown back in; feeling like a fraudulent imposter among these seasoned and well trained swimmers. Just now fully realising the mental and physical hurdles I'd have to overcome, if I were to have any hope of setting foot in France. A booming laugh from across the beach made me look up from my private pity party. It came from a swimmer with the most amazing smiley hat.

Have you ever seen a smiley and not smiled at it? It's impossible. You can't be sad in a smiley hat or when looking at one. I smiled at the silly hat with the silly face. I didn't know the swimmer and they were unaware that seeing their hat made all the difference to my grey day. From that point forward, mental preparation became as important as physical. I acquired a hat and with it a new online community of fabulously positive and encouraging people. People I'd never met but who wanted me to succeed anyway. Before every big training swim I practised the same routine. Browse through motivational images, read quotes that motivate and inspire me. Steady my heart and my mind for the task ahead. Put on my smile and finally, my smiley hat, to hold all that lovely positivity in.

My 'happy cap' and I were inseparable buddies in the months leading to my Channel swim and there was only one choice when I got 'the call' from my escort boat pilot telling me my time had come.

It was calm and sunny when I put on my (now magical) red Happy Wild Swimming cap and let the encouragement, experience, love, family and positivity it was imbued with, fuel me south to France.

I'm a happy Channel swimmer with the best certificate 7 year old me could have ever hoped for.

NB: Lucy was the first female to swim the English Channel solo wearing a 'happy cap'

Mind, Body & Siesta Key

Nicole Buckley

I am a swimmer. I honestly can't remember a time I couldn't swim. My dad threw me into a pool at the age of two, the old fashioned 'sink or swim' test. I swam. I never feared the water. I have a hard time understanding why every person on earth doesn't love the water. To me, water is healing, water is soothing and water is the only place on earth that I don't hurt. Ah, now there's where my story really begins.

I swam all through my formative years on a swim team. I swam twice a day from the time I was 13 years old throughout high school. I competed at the national level within the YMCA (Young Men's Christian Association) in the USA. Every year I qualified to swim in Fort. Lauderdale, Florida and it was such a thrill to head to the tropical south to swim in that national swim meet. I was a swimmer, but only a pool swimmer. Also, I was a lifeguard and taught swimming lessons for many years. I especially loved working with children under the age of 3 who had no fear of the water.

That's the beginning of my life in water. Life happens though. My life began having consequences that weren't always the best. I stopped working out in the water and tried an array of 'land sports'. I had some excess weight issues after the birth of my first daughter and decided that I didn't want to be overweight. While I was in nurses training, I lost over 100 lbs through severe diet and exercise. I maintained that lost weight over five years. I became pregnant and regained about 60 lbs immediately. My husband and I decided to relocate to Florida, instead of waiting until retirement. This will become one of the best decisions I made in my life. I had some pretty intense blows to my life. The first was a divorce. Then I had a nervous breakdown and was diagnosed bi-polar.

I was placed on medication for my mania and within six months I gained over 150 lbs. My parents were both morbidly obese and with my previous history of being overweight, my body reacted in this unfortunate way. I was a single mom, stressed, overworked, always worried, depressed, sad and could barely find the energy to live day to day life, much less work out. My eating habits were horrendous, mainly fast food. Over the next 13 years I gained more and more weight. I'd diet, lose 10 lbs then gain 15 lbs. It was an endless battle. I was working 12 hour shifts in hospital.

An intervention was done on me by my place of employment. I lost my job. I lost my career. I was encouraged by my primary doctor to have weight loss surgery. I had met 'my bottom'. The one alcoholics or drug addicts reach to finally begin recovery. I weighed in at a massive 380 lbs. I was using a wheelchair for ambulation in the community. I used walkers and canes within my home. I was doing NO physical activity. I was very sick, physically, emotionally and spiritually. My legs were so severely damaged from end stage arthritis that they had locked into a 45 degree angle. No orthopedic surgeon would operate because the chance of recovery from bilateral knee replacements was so poor.

I underwent Roux-N-Y Gastric Bypass surgery over 7 years ago. I was going to be given a second chance. I followed every rule that my registered dietician and surgeon gave me. I began psychological counseling weekly. I was unable to walk. Thus began my re-entry to the pool. I would go to the pool for 2-4 hours and walk back and forth. I'd tread water and do aerobics. Eighteen months later I was 240 lbs lighter. I was freed from obesity.

I felt so wonderful that I decided I didn't need to have my knees replaced. They were fused into a bent position but I could swim. I began swimming laps. I swam daily. My sister sponsored me to swim in an open water event, swimming the portion of a triathlon with her husband. Thank goodness he dislikes swimming. Because I was a pool swimmer, I knew I needed to

transition to ocean swimming. I joined a local triathlon club and enjoyed practicing with my new buddies each time they swam. The experience of swimming in the sea transformed me. No longer did I itch from the chlorine. I found I wasn't tired after swimming in the ocean, instead I was invigorated. I loved swimming with the dolphins and fish. After the competition that I did in Miami, Florida, I was hooked on open water swimming. The problem now became my legs. I had great difficulty getting to the beach. Canes and walkers don't do well in the sand!

I made the decision to have my knees replaced. It was the most painful thing I have ever done in my life. I will say that my recovery will never be 100%. Because I waited so long to have the surgery my legs atrophied, I had severe osteoporosis which required large prosthetics. Also, I have only 90 degrees range of motion. My hamstrings were cut to lengthen my legs. I am six inches taller than before surgery and 1/2 inch taller than high school, as my surgeon repaired my bowed legs. Now I have very straight legs. Within 6 weeks of surgery my surgeon told me I could return to the sea. I usually wear fins to encourage my legs to kick. I wear 'heavy' fins which do not float and I'm happy to say my leg muscles have recovered from the severe atrophy. Unfortunately, as I previously mentioned, the only place my legs and back do not hurt is in water.

Let's talk about where I am over two years later from my knee surgeries. I swim 5-7 times a week in the sea. I have set many goals and achieved each and every one of them. This past winter, because of social media and my friends across the 'great big blue' who are enamoured with cold water swimming, I acclimatised to swimming in water at 53 degrees F. That was huge for me. I do use neoprene booties, hat, footies, and a wetsuit. I have severe peripheral vascular issues and become severely numb in my extremities. Yet, I have found that my beautiful sea brings many elements that challenge me, yet make me feel whole.

Each day, I begin in the sea. I meditate. I feel that the healing I've received comes from the sea, salt and the very original 99.9% white quartz sand that I am blessed to have at Siesta Key, Sarasota, Florida. I have surrounded myself with amazing people, who love the ocean as much as me.

I honestly believe that the sea has healed me. Am I perfectly healed? No, of course not. I have to spend so much energy maintaining my well being. I see my therapist. I eat healthy. I mediate. I live my life so simply. But, most importantly, I swim. I immerse myself in the salty turquoise waters daily. This is where I have found peace, tranquillity and serenity. Ok, I will admit, it's hard to see my body (sometimes) with the excess skin, scars and varicose veins. Then I remind myself, my body is telling a story - one of recovery, hope and gifts. I am blessed.

Scilly Over Arm Stroke

Carol Tolfrey

Having been born and lived on Tresco Isles of Scilly until I was 15 years old, I've done some pretty wild swimming.

I learnt to swim in the sea when I was about 5 years old. I loved growing up on Tresco it was a perfect childhood with about 35 children in the whole school.

We didn't wear goggles or hats in those days and certainly not wetsuits! Yet we swam all year round, doing what we called 'over arm' stroke.

My favourite beaches on Tresco are Pentle Bay, Appletree Bay and Rushy Bay but it really is hard to choose as all the beaches are fabulous. One place that sticks in my mind where we played was called Piper's Hole. It is a sea cave at the north end of Tresco which opens into a freshwater pool. We used to bravely climb down into the cave but then get very scared.

I didn't learn how to swim front crawl until 9 years ago, aged 62, when I was going to enter my first triathlon event and my son, Neil decided to learn crawl too. He had already completed several triathlons prior to this but all were achieved swimming 'head up in the air' breaststroke style. Since then he has gone on to successfully complete three Ironman triathlons and I have completed 11 triathlons myself.

I love swimming during all the different holidays we've had, one of them being the Great Barrier Reef which was fantastic as were Dubai and this year in Cape Verde.

For convenient changing and warmth, I bought Neil a Happy Wild Swimming Dryrobe as a surprise last year and myself one too. They are ideal as we swim in the open sea, three or four times a week, at Eastney beach in Southsea.

Many of the regulars who swim there are often seen sporting Happy Wild Swimming caps, in various colours. They certainly keep the spirits up and make us look a happy bunch!

Photos: (left) Holiday Cape Verde beach; (right) Fun at Eastney beach

The Singing Swimmer

Jody Jones

In 2011, I gave birth to a beautiful baby girl and 6 months later decided to leave my teaching career behind me after 16 years to create more of a work-life balance. My husband was a Major in the Army and we were living on the beautiful Jurassic coast in rural Dorset. In early spring 2012, a few months before the Olympics took the country by storm, I decided that I was feeling a little bit lost and turned to my husband one day and told him that I wanted to go for a swim in nearby Lulworth Cove. He thought I was a little mad but went along with it and so I donned my kayaking wetsuit, pink hat and goggles and took the plunge. Whilst I slogged my way across the cove, he kept a close eye on me from the stony beach with our daughter in the toddler rucksack on his back, until I dragged myself out of the water after about 400 metres – feeling very unfit but with the biggest smile. I was hooked.

The next thing I knew I had entered myself into a 1 mile open water swim in Poole in September and had hired a proper triathlon wetsuit. I trained in the cove at weekends and in the pool during the week. I was shocked at how rubbish my swimming had become – I had been a competitive club swimmer as a kid but had stopped when I was about 14, not swimming properly again until I was at university, after which I stopped again. I completed my mile sea swim in just over 40 minutes and was elated! Within a year I took part in the Dart 10k and swam from Alcatraz across San Francisco Bay. I'd also met a lot of hugely inspirational and very kind people from the open water swimming community. Marathon swimming was definitely the way forward for me.

Open water swimming had become a huge part of my life and a place where I could go to think about things or switch off if I needed to. I would reluctantly get out of the water but always felt happy and content.

So, when I heard about the Facebook group 'Happy Wild Swimming' I quickly jumped on board and bought my 'happy cap'.

I will swim pretty much anywhere – lakes, rivers, the sea – and do so at every available opportunity, all year round. I feel very privileged to be able to swim in these beautiful places and experience nature close up and in a way that people who never venture into open water will ever get to see. In the last few weeks alone I've seen rays on the sea bed in Bournemouth, more herons than I can count, countless fish of various shapes and sizes, a grebe swimming around with a fish in its beak, a seal and most special of all, a kingfisher.

Two years ago, when I was pregnant with my second baby, during a post-swim chat over a cup of tea and a bacon roll with a swimming friend, we came up with the idea of putting an English Channel relay team together. As young club swimmers, my lane mates and I always used to brashly declare that one day we would swim the English Channel. It was never something that I ever thought I would actually be in a position to do in reality. Yet here we were sowing a little seed of an idea. Two months later I booked our pilot and tide slot for July 2016 and we were in the process of putting a team together. The wetsuit was well and truly ditched. In the run up to the swim I had my baby, swimming right up to the week before she was due and then had to build up my distances again. I entered the Chillswim Coniston End to End (5.25 miles) and the Henley Bridge to Bridge 14.1km swims in 2015 to give me a goal. Also, I started swimming with an amazing group of swimmers at Durley Sea Swims in Bournemouth – a group of successful and aspiring Channel relay and solo swimmers. On 14th July 2016, our team, the aptly named 'Missed the Ferry' Channel relay team successfully reached France. We landed just round from Cap Gris Nez, the point where swimmers try to aim for, to be greeted by Bastille Day revellers who gave us a standing ovation from the cliff top and a very welcome glass of champagne each. Tradition denotes that upon reaching France, swimmers must choose a pebble as a memento – I picked up two. One for me and one for my husband without whom I would not have been able to train and who supports me in all that I do. Marathon swimming is never truly a solo event. Our swim, under the guidance of our brilliant pilot, Paul Foreman on his boat 'Optimist', was completed in 13 hours, 58 minutes and 40 seconds. There were tears but they were very happy tears and the biggest smiles ever!

My next big challenge was with Chillswim attempting to swim the length of Windermere, England's largest lake at 10.5 miles long. I proudly wore my Happy Wild Swimming cap for this swim.

Although I felt very nervous about it, I knew how hard I had trained. So despite not having the best of weather conditions I successfully completed this swim in 7 hours and 30 seconds! I used this swim as a stepping stone towards what will be my next challenge.

A year ago at Durley, when completing my 2 hour qualifying swim for the relay, one of the most generous and inspiring swimmers that I know, motivated me to take the next step in my Happy Wild Swimming journey. Within a week, I was back on the phone to Paul Foreman booking my English Channel solo slot for August 2018.

What I've omitted so far is that between December 2013 and May 2014, my husband and I lost 3 babies, a singleton and a complicated twin pregnancy at 14 weeks. My husband was training for several ultramarathons at the time which helped him to start the healing process and to take his mind off things. As well as finding solace with each other and our daughter, my therapy came from being in the water and from singing with the lovely ladies in my choir, a branch of over 75 Military Wives Choirs. Miscarriage is a devastating blow that is often not discussed, but being around these amazing women, who have such tumultuous lives with postings, deployments, family upheaval and of course loss, really helped me through. I will always have a special place in

my heart for my choir sisters – we have an incredible bond and I love them dearly. Swimming gave me focus, helped to wash away my sadness and I began to find my drive again. The Channel relay and planning for my Windermere swim also helped to get me back on track.

Whilst I now have my beautiful second baby, there will always be a part of me that feels sad. However, I am happy and life is good. I have a wonderful husband, 2 beautiful daughters, 2 very silly spaniels, wonderful friends, my choir, swimming and the knowledge that I am a Channel Relay Swimmer with more big challenges to come.

Every swimmer has their reason for swimming.

Whether in the pool or open water, in a wetsuit or without, chatty heads up breaststroke or marathon swimming.

My reason is purely because

it brings me joy!

A Journey Of Miles

Miles Redhead

The great sporting loves in my life have always been swimming, running and fishing. As long as I can remember my ambitions were always to run a marathon and swim the English Channel.

I was first taken swimming by my dad when I was around 3 years old, to the Marine Spa in Torquay. Those Sunday morning sessions ended abruptly when one day I allegedly dropped my swimming trunks on the pool side and weed into the pool. I am not sure if we were banned or if Dad was too embarrassed to ever take me again!

Around the same age whilst on a holiday to La Toja in Spain, I managed to make my way onto the top diving board of an Olympic sized outdoor swimming pool (irresponsible parents?) and scared my mum so much she never went near the water again.

Later, I was professionally taught to swim by Ray Bradbury at The Palace Hotel in Torquay. He was a fantastic swimming coach.

At a similar time, my dad took us fishing for the first time off the rocks at Institute Beach.

Wrasse and Blenny fish were in abundance and you caught one every cast – the perfect activity for kids with the attention span of a gnat. To pardon the pun, I was hooked!

I have spent many hours over my lifetime fishing around the bay, but those rocks have always been my favourite spot.

At school, I was always in the swimming teams. Firstly, at Montpelier school in Paignton, where in my final year I broke several school records - only for my brother to beat them all 2 years later! (For which I have secretly hated him ever since).

Aged 12-18, I attended Kings College, Taunton. Every summer I was in the swimming and water polo teams. During my school holidays at home I also swam locally and was briefly in the Torquay Leander swimming club. I remember swimming in a gala at the open-air swimming pool at Newton Abbot, (which has now gone in place of the Sainsbury's on the Penn Inn roundabout). I was about 14, but was placed in the men's category and I got absolutely thrashed - which did me no harm as it just made me try harder to not be beaten next time.

Aged 26, I joined the Army and over the next 14 years, swam in various regimental swimming and water polo teams. During this time, I got more into running as the Army involved quite a lot of it. I had run several half marathons over the following years, but then was diagnosed with arthritis, aged 36. This scuppered all hopes of a full marathon ever happening.

As the running stopped, the weight increased. So I switched from running to swimming. Firstly back in the pool and then I saw a 1 mile charity sea swim advertised in Teignmouth raising funds for the local Rowcroft Hospice. I swam this with my daughter and really enjoyed it. A few weeks later I swam the Agatha Christie Mile from Goodrington to Broadsands. I was hooked.

Shortly after that, I joined the Outdoor Swimming Society and saw the Dart 10k advertised - the aquatic equivalent of a marathon. I thought if I can't run one I will swim one! Over the summer of 2011, I trained solidly

in the pool and in the sea at Broadsands Beach. In 2011, I achieved my goal by successfully swimming the Dart 10k and did so again in 2012. Though I decided not to swim it a third time as it took so much time to train it had overtaken my home life.

In 2013, I saw a Pier to Pub swim advertised in memory of a swimmer who died swimming that summer. I registered for it and at registration got talking to a couple called Gary and Claire, who were new to sea swimming, entering this one as their very first (and as it turned out, only) sea swimming event.

In 2014, I joined Facebook and discovered a local group called Happy Wild Swimming. A post said they were swimming that weekend at my favourite 'fishing' location of Institute Beach, so I went along. It was a pleasant surprise to discover it was Gary and Claire who had organised the swim. Having previously met them as they prepared to enter their first sea swim just months before, it was nice to meet up again as I stood on the beach ready to join a new group.

The swim was to be in the sea, passing the rocks where Dad took me all those years before. As I swam past my favourite fishing spot, I wondered why on earth the idea of jumping in and swimming had never occurred to me?

Since that very first swim, we have now swum most of the bay.

We swim all year round as a group and in January this year, Gary and I swam at night with just torches lighting up our tow floats, otherwise swimming into darkness, which was strangely enjoyable.

In 2014, although he couldn't swim that distance at the time, Gary arranged for those who were capable of doing so, to swim 4km from Torquay Harbour to Paignton Harbour. He wore his happy cap while kayaking as safety support.

Some swimmers also swam back the majority of the way too, with Claire and Linda, (probably the two shortest in the group), completing the whole two way swim (8km). One way was enough for me, but a most enjoyable achievement in my home location.

We've had many other good times too. In 2015, we had a fantastic weekend at Bigbury-on-Sea. We swam over a mile in the sea around

Burgh Island one day, followed the next day by a 6km river swim from Aveton Gifford to Bantham, including the notorious 'swoosh' section.

Other swims include around Thatchers Rock one evening, in challenging 'rip tide' type currents. I was happy Gary had organised a speedboat owned by fellow swimmer Patrick, as safety cover. Although it was never required it was great comfort to all swimming.

A more recent highlight was when we swam to a natural arch near Torquay harbour (known locally as London Bridge) to enter hidden caves. I was staggered at the marine life on the walls and the difference between the usual high tide view and what the low tide revealed.

Nowadays, my arthritis means I will never realise my 2 ambitions. But who cares? I am enjoying new challenges every swim!

I Swam Out Into The Road

Karen Saltwell

I'm lucky enough to live in a little old mill house. It's built above ground level and part of my house is actually built into the river. The house is small but the grounds cover three acres.

Living alongside the river for just over 17 years I've seen the river rise and fall many times. Sometimes the river has burst its banks and the land that surrounds our house floods. I'm used to this. We move our cars up to the local pub, put wellies on, put anything that is ground level up and we wait for it to go down.

A couple of times in the past, the water has risen so high it's been on our decking and our hearts are in our mouths. Once being one Christmas Eve and another Christmas Day ... oh what fun that was!

23rd June 2016, it had been raining very hard during the night. We woke to find the water had started to creep onto the lawn. My boys who are usually around were at Glastonbury so were not able to help gather the garden furniture and everything that was ground level to put up to a safe place. My husband and I set to and before long everything was up outside the house. We have decking areas in other parts of the garden that are very high and keep our things out of harm's way.

This particular day the water kept rising. We were worried it might come in the house. So we lifted everything we could up off the ground, taking what we could to the bedrooms to minimise the damage if it came in.

Well, it did start to come in. Absolutely nothing more could be done.

So what would any swimmer do in this situation? I got in and had a swim!

I put my wetsuit, happy wild swimming hat and goggles on and swam lengths up and down my driveway; my drive is over 50 metres long.

I went into the back garden where the water was really deep in parts. When I stood up the water was around my neck. In another part of the garden, the river was coming down with such force it was like swimming in a never ending pool. I was having great fun.

I decided to go back down the drive and swam out into the road. When I stood up there was a van to the left of me with a man on the roof. He had tried to cross the river and had broken down. The water was halfway up the van. Another guy was trying to push the van back out. When I looked to my right there was a gathering of neighbours. They had come along to look at the flooding and to see if they could help with the van. They all thought it hilarious that I'd been swimming in the garden and even funnier that I was in my wetsuit.

I think it's a day we will all remember for many different reasons.

Yes, the water came in but we didn't have much damage apart from a few loose floor tiles and loose skirting boards. A little touch up with paint and you wouldn't know anything had happened - I'd enjoyed a unique swim!

Isle Of Arran Adventures

Jock Bagnall

Here goes fine fellows ...

Being born on the Isle of Arran, Scotland, and just 30 yards from the sea, I suppose swimming became 'our thing to do' in the late 1950's and 1960's. One could not wish for a better place to swim, living in Lamlash (*An t-Eilean Àrd*).

When we were in our early teens, we used to swim across and around the Holy Island. It was great for swimming and sometimes we would camp on there. The water was always so clear in and around the Island, we just loved diving off the rocks and getting in by the lighthouse.

One unique thing we used to do, quite regularly, was to wait for when the basking sharks came in close in order to swim with them. Believe it or

not, our grandfathers even used to fish them. We didn't, instead we did something our fathers used to do. As the sharks would ply up and down the Firth of Clyde, feeding with their mouths open wide, cruising along on the surface, we would swim up from behind them. Their rear fin would stick out of the water, so if we could, we'd attach ourselves to the fin and get pulled along. The game was to see who could go the furthest while holding on. We must have looked so small alongside these huge sharks, some often measuring up to 15 or 20 feet long!

Fortunately basking sharks are almost completely harmless. Well, almost. The sharks knew we were holding on so, like submarines, they would just slowly head down to the deep. Of course, the adventure for us was to hold on like blazes, until they came to the surface again. Most of the time they did and so did we. When they didn't our lungs would be bursting so we would have to let go at the last second to have enough air to swim back up. No goggles or ear plugs in those days. Sounds mad, it was!

Other times, the sharks would sway, or just flick their rear fin which we were holding onto and whoosh, off we would go! Many times, we would be swimming past the lighthouse holding onto the sharks and the lighthouse keeper, called McGregor, would give us an eerie eye. Through time we got to know him and he was actually a fine chap.

Looking back, I'd have to say we had a great time. Some people may say, "Silly youths!" but I think not. Funnily enough, I and my three mates all ended up as Marine Engineers, with one, Murdo, getting his M/Mariner ticket. All, like me, still swim regularly despite being in our 70's now!

These days I'm accompanied by my 'Crew' (great grandchildren). It is a joy to see them happy swimming at such a young age.

From Pool

To Poole

Elizabeth Verth

Just over two years ago, I was confined to the four walls of a swimming pool. If I was really lucky, it was a 50 metre pool ... and if I was really, really lucky, that pool a beautiful outdoor one in Sydney, Australia. I thought then that I was truly blessed and very happy, having recently rediscovered the joy of swimming.

Then, one evening in early 2014, whilst visiting Sydney from my home near Poole in Dorset, I was trawling Facebook and found a well known swimming group. Oh, for goodness sake! Thrilling or what?!! An online community, for swimmy people, by swimmy people, who completely amazed me with their swimming talents and exploits. Enter Sally Bird.

Even with the wonders of the World Wide Web, there is still something exhilarating about being online and bumping into someone from your home town, especially when there is 10,000 miles between you. So excited was I to see a posting from this lady, I replied immediately, asking: "Where do you swim in Poole? I'm in Australia at the moment, but I'd love to meet up when I get back in the spring" ... thinking then that she would suggest a municipal swimming pool. Her reply? ... "In the sea!"

She had to be joking. For goodness sake, it was February! The sea temperatures were barely topping 5C along the Dorset coastline. This woman must be completely mad, truly 'off her trolley' in a completely 'nuts out of her head' kind of way. Sally went even further. She sent me a request to join her Facebook open water swim group "Beyond the Blue". I pressed the accept button quite tentatively, wondering what was about to befall me. Over the next few months, from the heat of a Southern Hemisphere summer, I watched the exploits of mad-cap people from this English outdoor swimming group, shaking my head in disbelief at their utter madness and being amazed by the sheer joy of their winter swimming playtimes in the freezing waters of Poole. I thought that I might wander down and check them out in the summer.

My first foray into the English sea at Poole came a little earlier than I had anticipated.

It was on a beautiful sunny day in mid-May.

Following a whole series of frustrations at my local pool, I decided it was time to take the leap of faith ... into the sea. No more walls.

So it was that I met Sally Bird and fellow Beyond the Bluers at Shore Road. My biggest concern was the cold. Being an expatriate tropical baby, I suffered badly in cold conditions and was terrified I wouldn't be able to cope or, even worse, that I would make a complete fool of myself. The ever prepared Sally brought down neoprene socks and gloves for me to wear and suggested that I double cap. Off I went into the sea, squealing with delight, terror, pain and bravado. It was so very cold and so very lovely. Just so much fun!

The sea had opened a door to adventure. My inner child came out to play. I was hooked.

Since those early heady days of my romance with the sea, I have embraced the open water with the joy that it has extended to me. I've never been very sporty, but all that has changed now. No more walls. Thanks to Beyond the Blue, I really have gone from pool to Poole.

For the first time in my life I have a sport which I love, one that I can call my own. Taking part in swim events is another new experience, each one of which has presented me with a new and greater challenge.

My Big Swim Adventure during 2016 was a successful relay swim across the English Channel with team "Missed the Ferry", a group of mildly eccentric likeminded swimming nutters. We did it! I almost have to pinch myself to check that I'm not dreaming.

To say that open water swimming has changed my life is not an exaggeration.

Joining Happy Wild Swimming was a natural extension of my new open water swimming activity. It gives me great joy to wear their smiley badge and to live their very apt slogan of "Swimming with smiles".

Page opposite: A mix of happy swimmers having fun by the sea and river in Devon, Dorset and Sussex.

Swim Every Day In August

Lucy Stansfield

To be honest I don't remember how I was invited to join Lorna Macgregor's challenge but it immediately struck me as the sort of thing I wanted to be part of. Having to swim in open water every day in August felt more like heaven than a challenge. I'd have the perfect excuse for going out every day. I decided to make it a little more fun by swimming at a different location in Orkney each day and to swim with as many people as I could.

I regularly swim with the Orkney Polar Bears and they were key to me identifying where and when to swim. I have about a dozen regular places to swim but ended up with a list of over 40 potential spots. Here are a few of my personal challenge statistics:

32 swims - 31 in the sea and 1 in a reservoir
1 night swim
Only 2 swims on my own and the biggest group was 9 swimmers
A total of 28 people swam with me and to my surprise, and awe, this included 2 Channel relay swimmers
3 families on holiday joined in as did 3 other holidaymaking swimmers
3 Polar Bears completed the challenge too, although we didn't always swim together due to work and family commitments

I began the month really concerned about finding 31 locations where I felt safe to swim. Although I am always careful to check tide times and the weather before swimming, the dozen or so places I swam before the challenge were well known to me. I had to quickly learn a lot more about tides, currents, etc. in places I had never even visited let alone swum at. By the end of the month my confidence in being able to use this information was much improved.

However, inevitably there was the day I totally failed to plan. I arranged a trip to the Brough of Deerness and a lovely swimming spot was promised by everyone who'd already swum there. Three intrepid Polar Bears risked the curiosity of tourists and gulls alike as we walked across the path and climbed down to the water. What water I asked myself. It was low tide and we could barely see it and we couldn't work out how to get in as the usual entry points were now above the sea level. Two of us were seriously considering going back to swim elsewhere that day when our braver

friend just went for it and launched into the very cold water. She had the exit point worked out already so off we went into the channel towards the sea. The weather and tide didn't allow us to swim right out but it was incredible looking up at the cliffs full of gulls. After a while I looked up only to see a crowd (OK it was only about a dozen people) at the top of the cliffs, cameras in hand. This made getting out of the water and changed more interesting than usual.

Looking back this was the most amazing month and genuinely changed me. I have made new friends, visited new places, beaten fears and improved my health and wellbeing. I have jumped waves, swum with seals, swum across to a holm (island), swum there and back to another,

swooshed under 4 bridge arches, 3 at the Brig of Waithe near Stromness and 1 in Finstown, had to use suntan lotion in Orkney and been joined by my amazing grandsons (5, 3 and 6 months at the time). I have swum in harbours, a reservoir, from beaches, from rocks, from private islands and slips.

I have laughed more than I thought possible. Especially at Aikerness in the haar (cold sea fog) and at the 4th Churchill Barrier when the waves were big and the tide was coming in fast with the jellyfish seeming to chase us wherever we went. This swim was followed by a quick look for the Orca whales which had been spotted around the area the day before and the luxury of a rare hot chocolate with 2 fellow Polar Bears.

I swam in brilliant sunshine, pouring rain, thick haar, strong winds and everything else apart from hail and snow. The most beautiful day for me was at East Side in South Ronaldsay (above) when the sun was strong enough to warrant suntan lotion! I used to live near this beach but had never swum there and wish I knew why. It was a day when swimming in the sea, with a panoramic, deserted beach to look at and with wonderful company meant nobody wanted to leave the water. Sadly, we had to get out in the end. The sea temperature was about 13C and without wearing our wetsuits, the thought of hypothermia setting in was on our minds.

It is so difficult to decide which my favourite swim was and which I liked the least as every swim was truly a pleasure.

If I had to choose, the 2 least favourites would have to be Hatston slip in Kirkwall and Houton purely because they are in more developed areas. However, it surprises me that my 'local' spot in Stromness harbour is equally developed yet I love swimming there with the views of Hoy in the distance. (Above: The Point Of Ness, Stromness; Below: Stromness Reservoir)

My favourite swims would have to be Evie, where I never cease to be astounded by the way the sea and sky change from minute to minute and Inganess Bay in Kirkwall, where we regularly swim around the wreck there as planes take off from the airport less than 400m away.

In the few weeks since the challenge ended I have swum every day apart from one when the weather made it unsafe. I have revisited several of the places I went to for the first time in August. Best of all, every day is a smiling, Happy Wild Swimming day for me and I can honestly say I smile before, during and after every swim!

Above: Swimming in The Cannon, Stromness; Below: Skipi Geo, Birsay.

For Adventure And Pleasure

Monica Brogan

I believe that I was destined to be a happy wild open water swimmer even before I was a twinkle in my mother's eye.

My mom told us how her dad, a World War I veteran, went down in a diving suit in the Philippines to retrieve the ship's anchor which had been lost during a typhoon. He also swam the Carquinez Strait to settle a bet at a Navy picnic.

My parents were married at the end of World War II in Watsonville, California and honeymooned at Carmel-by-the-Sea. My dad swam in the era of Jack LaLanne (the godfather of modern fitness) at the Sutro Baths, a large public saltwater swimming complex in western San Francisco.

I was born not far away within a few miles of Ocean Beach. Appropriately, my Zodiac sign is Aquarius. We went to the beach for picnics just below the Cliff House.

Photo: With my mom & sister, grandmother in background

My first memories of outdoor swimming are family fly fishing trips, accompanied by Nana T, my dad's mom. Every year we drove up to Downieville, California, where my dad made a pool of river rocks for my sister Therese and I to swim in the North Fork of the Yuba River. I suppose the water was cold, but despite that we couldn't wait for Daddy to make our pool so we could swim like the trout ... which would be our lunch the next day if fishing went well.

CLEARLAKE HIGHLANDS

In 1961, we bought a cabin at Clear Lake and it is there that I really embraced outdoor swimming. In spring, the water was cold and clear. We squealed as we braved the waves and wind wearing just our swimsuits and swimming shoes – old tennis shoes repurposed to protect our tender feet. We swam through the summer, as the water warmed and the lake lowered to provide irrigation for the great Central Valley of California via Rumsey Creek outflow through the canyon.

We went out in the family boats through the years.

The first one had oars in case the outboard motor gave out, later a speed boat, then a sail boat – each time taking a packed lunch and fishing gear.

Sometimes we pulled in at quiet beaches for lunch and a swim. Other times we stopped in the middle of the lake and jumped fearlessly into the water to swim around the boat.

When I was in high school, I volunteered every summer teaching Red Cross Summer Swim lessons at Rossi Pool, 2 blocks from my house. We were also lucky to be able to enjoy the last years of Fleishhacker Pool, located next to the zoo in the southwest corner of San Francisco. It was the world's largest heated saltwater outdoor pool, measuring 1000 feet in length by 160 feet width in the middle, (approx 300 metres by 50 metres). It was designed to accommodate 10,000 swimmers, had diving platforms one end and was so large the lifeguards patrolled in rowing boats! Even the military used it for aquatic drills during the war years.

We often went to China Beach outside the Golden Gate to play in the waves, where the rocks rolled in the tide. I never joined a league and I never raced, instead I swam every weekend up at the cabin. I just swam for the adventure and pleasure of being out there. I taught others the joy of being at one with the water.

When Therese and I traveled to Europe in the summer of 1971, I was determined to swim at every beach we visited. My list includes: Ostia in Rome, Blue Grotto (a unique natural sea cave) in Capri – yes we jumped out of the boat again - Naples under the shadow of Mount Vesuvius, Ravenna on the Adriatic and Vouliagmeni Beach in Athens.

Most recently I have taken to swimming at Buckroe Beach in Hampton, Virginia, near my home and during the summer I swam on the Eastern Shore at Kiptopeke State Park. I also swim in Lake Erie at Hamburg Town Beach, New York.

In my time I have completed a couple of triathlons and it is the swimming element that drew me to the sport in the first place. I'm currently training for distance, hoping to achieve a relay of larger proportions in the future.

When I am out swimming in open water, I enjoy wearing my Happy Wild Swimming cap and using my Swim Secure drybag tow float, both keeping me visible and safe. I even modeled my swim gear at a Cystic Fibrosis fund raiser fashion show at the school where I teach and showed my class how the float works.

Mrs. Br

Also, when hurricane Joaquin headed our way, I wore my Happy Wild Swimming Dryrobe into school.

It came in very handy on a particularly cold, wet and windy day, even the Athletic Director, my Tri buddy, borrowed it to go out to our trailers – the kids loved it!

I cannot imagine a better place to swim than out in nature: stream, river, lake or ocean – there is no water more natural and precious than that given to us to treasure, preserve, and enjoy.

Every time I swim out in the sea I feel so connected to all my other swim friends around the world. I grew up in the era of pen pals, postcards, patience for the mail to come and paper ephemera.

I am so happy to be able to keep in touch with instant messages and pictures we can share at the touch of a phone or computer. I dream of splashing with them in person someday soon.

Thanks to Gary and Claire creating this book I've had a chance to share my love of 'walking out into the water' - the thrill and peach that come with that adventure.

Why I Swim

Charlie Stockford

Some of my earliest memories are of messing about in water and boats. So it was natural for me to feel like a mermaid whilst growing up. I always thought I was one, just without long blonde hair.

A busy career, husband and children came along and I lost the time and inclination to swim. Then I got sick, very sick. I was diagnosed at the age of 34 with ME or CFS and ended up in bed for nearly 2 years.

ME (Myalgic Encephalomyelitis) is a crippling invisible illness that 15 years ago wasn't understood. "Yuppie flu" was the closest anybody got to understand it. The pain was constant. I couldn't move and had to be helped just to get to the bathroom. Surprisingly the doctor prescribed

anti-depressants (Seroxat) which made me convinced I was going mad. I lived in a dark room, sleeping more than I was awake, couldn't cope with smells, loud noise or talking with people. My family were amazingly supportive and helped nurse me through the worst of it.

I started helping my body and mind to work again by managing to walk to our front gate (150m), it took 40 minutes but I did it.

I joked to my husband that one day I'd do a triathlon!

So that got me thinking ... to do a triathlon you need to be able to swim. Minimal impact and with the thought that I might find it calming and beneficial my family helped me to and from the swimming pool (I couldn't drive yet). Tiny, baby steps (5 minutes floating in the pool to start with as climbing in and out was enough) I managed, very slowly and with lots of relapses, over the next 10 years to build up my strength – mentally and physically – to where I am now, regularly swimming 5-6km a week.

Swimming feels so natural and so comfortable to me that I thought swimming in open water in the sunshine might help too. At first my body went into shock but once everything calmed down and my body got used to the water it became more and more energising and I came out of the water feeling calm and somehow restored.

I completed my first triathlon 2 years ago and burst into tears on the finish line. It was a massive achievement from 10 years hard work.

It has been a huge journey for me but swimming has kept me sane and given me a way to relax and keep my stress levels down. I know now that emotional and physical stress are the two key triggers that will make me relapse (i.e. put me in bed for a couple of days) so swimming keeps a check on my stress levels. I have learnt to live with my ME ... we coexist ... I will never beat it as I've learnt that it is part of me and occasionally I get reminders that I've pushed it too far.

I never dreamt I would swim 5km, swim around Durdle Door in the sea, compete in sea swimming races, do triathlons on a regular basis, train to run a ½ marathon, cycle 100km or train to be a Swim Coach and Fitness Instructor but I have. I may not be fast or be able to do as much as I'd like but I love swimming and how it makes me feel. I have met some amazing people who I don't think would have featured had I remained in the corporate high stress high salary world. ME has given me the opportunity to have a different life to the one I thought I was going to have and for that I am really thankful as I get to go swimming, a lot!

Tri And You

Will Succeed

Kathy Moore

Over a glass of wine one evening in September 2013, I found myself agreeing to do a sprint triathlon. "It will be a challenge! It will be fun!" Slight problem, I realised that I hadn't done any open water swimming since I was 15 years old and I am now just past 50 years.

My journey began. First, some lessons in the pool, then, at the lake with safety kayaks and finally in the sea. Through DYST I found my local group 'Beyond the Blue' and the all location Facebook group of 'Happy Wild Swimming'.

The encouragement and support I received from fellow swimmers in person or via Facebook was incredible. At times when I found myself struggling with my training it gave me a much needed extra boost.

I love wearing my various Happy Wild Swimming caps.

Different colours to match different costumes.

I take them wherever I go, just in case there's a chance to swim!

I went on to complete my first triathlon in 2014. After recovering from injury which hampered my training in 2015 I've enjoyed competing during 2016.

I never thought I'd hear myself say I swim all year round in open water, but I do and I love it! I feel part of a big swimming family. Sea conditions will dictate what I do. Sometimes I swim, sometimes I wave jump. Other times it's what I call swalking (walking in the sea) or swigging (jogging in the sea). Always it's fun.

Also, laughter and a few squeals when it's really cold. There is always hot chocolate and cake at the end. For me, Happy Wild Swimming and *"Swimming with smiles"* sums it up perfectly.

I Leave With A Smile

Richard Nuell

Surprisingly, I found it quite hard to define a favourite swim.

Favourite organised event? Most challenging organised event? Favourite local swim route with friends? Most challenging local swim with friends? A swim, organised or informal, that gave me the biggest delight at having conquered it? Even my favourite aquathlon comes into the equation.

The important thing for me is for every swim to be a happy swim and that I leave with a smile, as shown on various 'happy caps' I proudly wear.

My favourite organised swim is the 1.4 mile Bournemouth Pier to Pier. Organised on a huge scale, I find it faultless and unfussy with a great atmosphere.

The most challenging for me was the Agatha Christie Mile at Broadsands, Devon in 2013. This was unfinished business from my previous attempt which I failed to complete as I had simply not had enough experience of surface chop. In between swims, I went to North Wales for some coaching from Dan Graham. This meant I had no excuse not to complete the swim. I succeeded second time, but it was hard!

I should also mention the annual local Long Swim at Clevedon, Somerset, which I've done 3 times. Although only 0.8 miles and looks deceptively calm, it can be a real horror, as it's located in the home of the World's second highest tidal range. Clevedon is highly regarded as a training ground for Channel swimmers. Some of our hardcore regulars and visitors have recently undertaken Channel relays. One told me that if you can cope with Clevedon on a bad day, you can cope with anything the English Channel throws at you.

Above: Swimming at Clevedon Pier with the paddle steamer MV Balmoral

My favourite local swim route with friends has to be anywhere from the beach at Clevedon. Our group, jokily named Middle Yeo Surf Lifesaving Club has existed around 50 years, with some members now in their 70s and 80s. We swim all year round in the sea at a time dependent on high tide. If the tide is coming in, we swim towards the buoys and after if it has turned, we swim towards the pier. Many of the group are faster and more adventurous than me, so I often go off on my own, remaining within the beach area. Embarrassingly, members of the public sometimes assume we are in trouble, so the coastguard occasionally gets summoned.

The most satisfying swims completed include the Barnstaple River charity mile swim in 2013 where, having observed the fast flow beforehand, I said "No way!" However, the organiser said I'd be fine as he would get one of his safety crew to keep an eye on me. Needless to say, it went well, though trying to get back to the exit after overshooting it was an experience! The Chippenham River Swims (2013 & 2014) and the Shrewsbury Mile (2015) were also good.

My Swimtrek swim around Burgh Island went surprisingly well as safety crews were nearby. In 2013, I completed a superb charity swim in Wales, from Ferryside to Llanstephan, organised by the local lifeboat crew and this was my first estuary swim.

Of the 34 swim only events I've attempted, I'm ashamed to say that I failed with 5 of them, which I considered to be unacceptable to organisers and safety team. With two, I was inexperienced in realising how a calm sea on a beach can become choppy further out. My most embarrassing failure was caused by cramp through not having trained enough. Two of my failures affected me badly mentally and I still live with 'crampy thoughts' every time I go out for a swim. The silly thing is that considering how much swimming I do, fully blown calf cramp hasn't struck since 2014. I know it's all in my mind but nothing can shift it.

I've also enjoyed some cold swims. Swimming all year round in the sea and lake has prepared me to enter 5 cold water skins swim events. Just short ones, but I'm pleased to be regarded as 'mad' when I tell people what I do in the winter months.

In addition, I've always been a keen runner and I'm a great enthusiast for events where you swim, then run. I've done 30 Aquathlons since 2009. The toughest is The Devil's Aquathlon, based at Sandford Parks Lido in Cheltenham, held on the final day prior to winter closure in October. The pool heating has been off for a week and it's a 2km swim in the lido's 50m main pool, followed by a hilly 10km run along roads and trails up to the local viewpoint The Devil's Chimney on Leckhampton Hill and back again. Certainly Happy Swimming and Happy Running there!

Finally, I owe a huge debt of gratitude to Happy Wild Swimming and Beyond the Blue groups, where having a nice swim together as a group means what it says. We swim together, wait for each other and have fun, with plenty of opportunities to be silly. Why should kids have all the fun?

I just wish I lived nearer so I could visit more often.

First Swim To An Island

Simon Parkin

In 2014, after chats on Facebook and a move to Somerset, Gary arranged my first Happy Wild Swimming adventure as a 'swim to an island'.

The outdoor swims I had done prior to this swim had a slight element of not wanting to be there - whether that had been to finish a bit quicker or that I was cold and didn't like it and wanted to go home and have a cup of tea. They were all great experiences but I had a niggling feeling that something was missing: a certain amount of joy. My swim to an island changed all that and I've got a theory as to why.

I met up with Gary and Claire and members of Happy Wild Swimming, a group who go swimming purely for the joy of swimming outdoors. With their expert local and marine knowledge they knew when it was best to tackle the reasonably short but challenging swim to Shag Rock, over 400 metres from the beach. On the day we chose, the sea was lively to say the least, but with the beautiful sunshine it was hard to cry off.

Five of us waded into the waves and headed off towards the island. Okay, technically it's a rock not an island but a small landmass surrounded by water was a good enough definition for my challenge.

The water was a lovely clear blue-green and I was able to put my head in the water for longer than I ever have before to do the front crawl. The sea threw us up and down like we were on a rollercoaster, but thanks to Gary and Claire's positive light-hearted attitude I didn't feel scared at all, just exhilarated.

After 10 minutes or so we reached Shag Rock. The waves were really crashing against it and I didn't think we'd be able to actually land on it but, after some coercing from Gary, I managed to sit on a rock at the edge of the island with him and get the money shot before the lively waves pummelled us off our barnacled perch!

We swam round the island and reluctantly headed back to shore, covered in seaweed and scratches, but euphoric after our shared adventure.

A few months later and it was Halloween. I had just finished 3 weeks of solid work and I had just had a hectic day. I drove through rush-hour traffic down the M5 to Devon to meet the Happy Wild Swimming group for another swim - a Halloween night swim. I was late. I hadn't even had

time to get a costume. I got out of the car and straight into my wetsuit, barely able to talk with leftover stress from the day and drive, then followed the group in fancy-dress down onto the beach. It was just a quick swim - more of a wade for me. I had a quick go at crawl and it was very strange swimming in the dark, but not that different from usual outdoor swimming. Maybe it's because I close my eyes when I'm underwater?

Another happy swim completed, it was nice to have a drink with everyone afterwards. They're a great group to swim and socialise with.

So what put the joy into these swims? It wasn't particularly the scenery or the ticking off of another challenge - it was the company, the shared camaraderie and the positive, joyous attitude of all the swimmers.

Minimalistic Joys
Of The River

Elaine Giles

Having been encouraged by Gary to 'grab a drink' before putting pen to paper it would have been rude not to. I chose a significant bottle, a gift for getting to France with 'Missed the Ferry' Channel relay team.

I started open water swimming as I had a fear of lakes. Odd, I know, but probably one of my better decisions. So I started off clad in a wetsuit and began my open water journey.

One summer's evening, armed with the wild swim map, I discovered a gorgeous bit of river. It turned out to be the perfect spot and the start of my truly favourite place to swim.

The next challenge was to swim all year round. I decided to start dipping in all weathers, more often than not with long suffering swim buddy Tom. I managed to assess the water temperature using the F***-o-meter scale the more one says F*** as one gets in the colder it is!

We've shared many a shivery sweary swim in sometimes rubbish weather but nothing beats the buzz of a winter dip.

It is a beautiful spot in the River Lee, with kingfishers, crayfish and all sorts of amazing wildlife to see.

I take quite a minimalistic approach when swimming. I've ditched the wetsuit, can't be bothered with gadgets and don't care how far or for how long I swim. I get out when I'm ready!

I've always been quite comfortable with my swimming, until the challenge of joining a relay team to swim across the English Channel was proposed by my friend Jody. Being completely non-sea savvy, I took a little trip to the small seaside town of Frinton-on-Sea in Essex to get a taste of the sea.

My next sea swim was when I met up with the rest of the swimmers in the 'Missed the Ferry' relay team. Despite swimming in different locations, it turned out that five of us regularly wore Happy Wild Swimming caps.

Let's just say that the very first dip, climbing off the boat, left me ready to never get in the sea again! Fortunately, swim buddy on the day, Diz Verth, swam with me and thankfully my second sea dip was a bit more of a success. My journey of sea swimming was a long one, but along the way I got to meet lots of different and interesting people. The result of hard work by the whole team was that I, Jody, Diz, Jodi, Charlotte and Neil, successfully completed our Channel relay crossing.

Swimming in the sea was fun but the river is where I feel completely comfortable. Back in my favourite location, I have a little group of secret dippers and I love taking new dippers to explore the surroundings. It's a fantastic feeling when I see other swimmers sharing the joy of the river.

Sal's Long Day Out

Sal Minty-Gravett MBE

I'd like to share with you a few steps during my life which culminated in my longest swim to date – my long day out!

In 1975, I was 18 years old and successfully swam my first solo English Channel swim from England to France, unaware it would become the first of 7 crossings I would make by the age of 59.

10 years later in 1985, I returned again, intending to swim from France to England, but instead ended up completing my second England to France swim. After that swim I made a vow to get at least one France to England swim completed as soon as possible.

Fortunately, this happened on September 20th 1992. It took me 12 hours and 8 minutes to swim from Cap Gris Nez (the closest point of France to England) to Shakespeare Beach, Dover, England, on what was a textbook and wonderful swim in great conditions. It was very fortuitous timing as the following year, in 1993, the French Coastguards banned all France to England swims. The seed was sown because now the only way I could do a France to England swim was via a 2 way crossing (swimming it both ways as a double crossing).

However, life then changed for me following my third English Channel swim in 3 decades. On the back of it, I started my own swim school in 1993 and my personal training was put to one side for a very long time. For 10 years I ran a very successful swim school, Swimrite, here in Jersey, before I was 'head hunted' by Serco - who were coming to Jersey to run the new commercial public pool being built and due to open in 2003 – leading to Swimrite closing its doors in July 2003.

I started with Serco as the Aquatics Development Manager - running what has become the biggest teaching programme here in the Channel Islands. We currently have 1300 pupils of all ages and abilities. At the opening ceremony the management said that if I was to do a '2 way' they would sponsor it. The new business and new commitment was all time consuming, ruling my life and world. Training in earnest was a problem.

However, with my 'next decade' looming, I decided I would book another 1 way swim for 2005. Along with 5 other local swimmers I completed this in 13 hours and 31 minutes on July 29th. Serco Jersey paid for this swim. As I was approaching France, my pilot said if I wanted to turn around and swim back I could as I was in the correct place to do so, but as I had been so sick for the first 7-8 hours I decided to finish well and left the 2 way challenge for another time.

I did plan to attempt the 2 way in 2015 but another swimmer was in training for a 2 way in 2013 and it made sense to 'train together', so I booked mine for July 2013 - Serco paid for this swim also. As it turned out we never did train together that much as our working hours were totally different. When it came to the day, again, I was so ill for the first 9 hours I decided to complete a one way (17 hours and 48 minutes) and come out in good shape. The weather broke into a huge thunderstorm and if I had turned around I would have probably been taken out of the water. It simply was not my day to do the double.

So, I still needed to get the blasted 2 way done. I found a pilot, Neil Streeter on SUVA who could 'fit me in' on the number 3 slot at the end of August 2014. I found various donations to pay for the swim, most were anonymous. Disappointingly, I never even got to Dover - the winds were far too strong. The swim rolled over to early August 2015, a number 4 slot. I went to Dover for a week and never even got in the water due to hurricane winds - again!

So, for 2016 I was found a number 1 slot at the end of August, surely third time HAD to be lucky for me? Accommodation at Varne Ridge was booked and plans were now in place to 'get the job done' – finally!

I changed my working hours and started part time teaching from January 2016, so my life/work balance was vastly improved. I also stepped down after 27 years as President of the Jersey Long Distance Swimming Club (JLDSC). I had been one of the founder members in 1974.

So, 2016 was going to be the year ... and all about 'me'. I've never ever put myself first before and find this is very hard to do.

In the Queen's birthday honours list in June 2016, I was awarded an MBE for my services to swimming, the greatest honour in my life to date. Though I had to keep it secret for two months since I had got 'the call' on 21st April from the current Lieutenant-Govenor, His Excellency General Sir John McColl KCB, CBE, DSO.

So, the year started wonderfully. I don't work in school holidays anymore meaning I could swim and train to my heart's content whenever I wanted. It was fabulous and I felt so strong and happy too!

I was due to help a young Australian swimmer cross the English Channel early in August and also an Indian swimmer cross the Catalina Channel just after that. Both trips were wonderful and both swims completed successfully! Whoop!

Then, I came home and focused on me.

My accommodation in Dover was booked for 25-31st August, my Support Crew handpicked six months earlier would arrive in advance of when I was due to swim. My husband Charlie and I flew over on the 24th to stay with friends and to relax - a skill which I had mastered well this year - because I had time to do so.

A few days on, we moved into our accommodation and relaxed some more. I called my pilot Neil who thought my swim would happen between Sunday-Tuesday. Settled weather was coming in, so we got the Crew over on Saturday 27th to prepare and to get to know each other beforehand.

Jersey Crew of Cliff Golding, Graeme Lowe and Bianca Kempster flew over that lunchtime, joined by Tracy Clark from Norwich.

By Saturday night, over dinner, lifelong friends were made in preparation for my big adventure.

However, Sunday we awoke to the news that an inexperienced swimmer had lost his life trying to complete a Channel swim - tragic news - but it didn't affect me - I couldn't allow it to. It was a lovely relaxing day, buying swim foods and prepping with my Crew.

The 'call' came through whilst we were all having dinner Sunday evening. We needed to be at Dover Marina for 8am, to start swimming around 8:30am. So, a last minute chat about my feeds and I went to sleep early (with my ear plugs) and left the Crew to sort themselves out!

The big day had arrived and on 30 August 2016, exactly 41 years after my first Channel swim, I successfully completed my '2 way swim' - England to France, very briefly stopping on the beach to clean my teeth and re-grease before swimming back from France to England – in a total time of 36 hours and 26 minutes.

I am seriously proud of this achievement - but I have to say I could not have done this without the amazing boat crew, Neil Streeter, Sam Jones, Adrian Piddock and my most loving, caring and fun Support Crew.

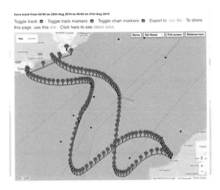

After my swim, I returned to a heroes welcome at Jersey Airport. It was the most amazing adventure. Something I will NEVER do again - I don't need to!

I feel that it took me a full 3 weeks of complete rest to be fully recovered. This was due to an ulcerated throat and mouth from all the sea water and my body needing to catnap very often. However, despite a little tendonitis in one forearm, I am completely uninjured. Not bad for an 'old bird'!

I simply love being in the sea and this swim has been 41 years plus of ocean swimming in the making, my ultimate challenge that I really needed to get down before I turn 60 next year. It means I have now completed 7 English Channel crossings - now for my book.

I really honestly believe that I was born to swim but have been forced to work ... and in the words of Capt. Matthew Webb, "Nothing great is easy". Nothing is more true ... and if it was easy, everyone would be doing it!

I am still raising funds for 2 wonderful local charities RNLI and Jersey Cheshire Homes. Here is my donation page should you be able to donate however small - it all helps: www.race-nation.com/sponsor/e/9207

My main and very important message to everyone reading this is to follow your dreams - whatever the size - live it - love it and enjoy it!

Just keep swimming ... and VERY happy (wild) swimming to you all!

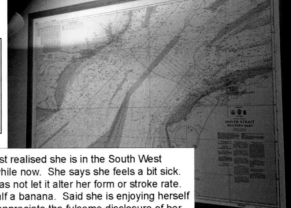

Above:

Dover Strait Chart

A present to Sal from husband Charlie

1247. Sally looks behind and has just realised she is in the South West shipping lane. She has been for a while now. She says she feels a bit sick. She has been sick a few times but has not let it alter her form or stroke rate.

1344. Feed of mint tea, CNP and half a banana. Said she is enjoying herself and doesn't currently feel sick. We appreciate the fulsome disclosure of her vomiting pattern!

1401. We spot our first compass jellyfish. Wind is dropping off now confirming that Neil made the right call to go this morning. Neil and his crew have a well-earned lunch.

1413. Sally is stung. "Oh f**k," she exclaims. "Stung me on my ear. Oh well," she laughs and swims on!!

1444. Feed – Muller rice and water. Two minutes later - "I just brought most of that up but I'm alright!" Sally asks to go onto half–hour feeds.

1515. Feed. Lots of jellyfish but she they don't faze her – been doing this too long to get freaked out by a few jellies. We are in the separation zone.

1545. Feed. Mint tea, CNP and half a banana. Sally says she feels a bit lightheaded and wants CNP on each feed. Wind is 10 knots. Water temperature 18-19C.

1604. We are nudging the North East lane at 7 hours 20 minutes. All good.

1615. Feed. Sally wants to take her mother's wedding ring off on the next feed! Mass panic. "You do it," we all say to each other. "You reach down and let her take it off and put it in a cup. No, you do it, I don't want the responsibility." The pressure was immense. What if it dropped into the sea?

1626. Captain Neil throws a small rubber duck at Cliff who, unprepared, took it full in the eye. Well, his glasses took the impact. The entire ship's company burst out laughing except Graeme who was horizontal on a break and quietly sleeping. Neil was laughing so much he sat down on a cushion holding his sides. Except it wasn't a cushion, it was Graeme. Neil didn't realise for a few seconds and then jumped up with a start. "Sorry Graeme, I thought you were a cushion!" Cue for lots more laughter. It's very tough on a two-way Channel swim?

1631. Sally sick again. The water temperature is19.2C.

1644. Heart stopping moment as Sally takes the wedding ring off and puts it into the largest bucket we could find which is attached to a reel! Tracy takes it and loudly tells Sally where it is for later. Sally says she is feeling sleepy. She has been swimming for 8 hours now.

1715. 850ft long Derby D passes in front of us followed soon after by a huge dredger bound for Immingham called Orca.

1720. Sally appears to be in that illusive place called 'the zone'. We plan to leave her for a bit. It is noticed by all of us that Sally seems to be in a happier frame of mind. The absolute enormity of what she is trying to do coupled with the memory of her previous attempt and the somewhat lumpy sea of the first several hours must have played on her mind. Also, she has struggled to 'let go', to cede control to Team SUVA and her own crew. But now it seems she has and in so doing has calmed down considerably. Now her crew feel more relaxed too. It's swim on!!

1730. Feed. We are going onto 45-minute feeds. Ideally we would like Sally to speed up her feeds (still averaging one minute or more). But it is difficult sometimes for the swimmer to achieve this. 45-minute feeds should help.

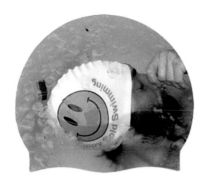

Swimming Under The Eiger

Shaun Hales

I checked my phone messages for the night and the intriguing line "want to go skydiving in Switzerland?" had appeared from my better half, Victorine. I can't remember the exact conversation but it was probably the usual "ok". Soon we found ourselves walking around the alpine town of Interlaken in the late hours looking for our lodgings, the crumpled print screened map was superbly useless, but I didn't mind exploring the streets in the crisp night air.

After a pleasant sleep we were greeted with a view of snowy peaks and blue sky, which we'd had no idea of when arriving in the dark the previous night. A bus to the airfield and a red jelly baby suit later we were standing on a helipad about to get high, the instructors were a laugh the whole time. We jumped in for the next flight and got the first dose of man up pills upon liftoff, or as it felt, blastoff. Flying past mountain peaks like ET and watching my partner disappear out the side door was probably the scariest thing I've seen. I donned my usual swim cap and jumped.

We turned to watch the helicopter disappearing above and then resumed our 'starfish' position, accompanied by 'dog head out the window' face. After a near vomit landing, we waved our goodbyes.

Next we took the train up towards Jungfrau, the same train which goes through the mountain used to ascend the infamous Eiger. If you have seen the film 'The Beckoning Silence' you know the importance of this mountain and its deadly north face. There was only one thing you can do in such an amazing place, swim!

We got off before Jungfrau, the highest station in Europe and crunched up the snowy hill to find a holding pond used for the snow cannons, most excellent. With no one else around and no one to stop us, we slid down the steep banks into the cool 4 degrees water, which was crystal clear and quite surreal.

Not an hour ago I was fast falling through the air, now I'm swimming under the north face of the Eiger!

That really eventful and yet casual morning, is still to be beaten - but I can try!

Giving It
A Go

Tracy Ranwell

When my friends Tina and Luke told me they had met Gary and Claire and a group of people who regularly swim in the sea local to me, I thought no more about it. Except, that was not the end of it - oh no! They said they were going and would I like to come along too. "In the SEA?!" I replied. "Go on!" they said, "You will love it; you have to be scared sometimes to know you're alive, ha ha".

The decision was made and we set about purchasing wetsuits, Happy Wild Swimming caps and a bright orange floatation 'thingy'. I liked the idea of having a rubber ring to hang on to!

The day was arranged for my first swim and so with bags of enthusiasm from Gary, Claire and others in the group, we all entered the water. Oh no, it was cold! What had I let myself in for? I was soon encouraged to let some cold water flush into my wetsuit, trapping it between my body and my wetsuit, to help keep a layer of warmth. A few screams and exclamations, then in everyone went. I held back. Fear, reticence, you name it; I just thought 'What am I doing? I am not the strongest of swimmers and I definitely do not enjoy being out of my depth'.

Before I knew it, I was flailing around in the water, yet somehow swimming forwards. Soon after, we had made it to the sea caves. I was scared, yes, but I had made it! I didn't know it before but wearing a wetsuit helps to keep you afloat. This was a welcome bonus as well as keeping me

warmer. Now all I had to do was swim back to the shore. I felt worn out but at the same time both exhilarated and incredible.

Did I mention the seaweed and fishy things? Well, they made me catch my breath more than a few times, but Gary and Claire were really understanding and helpful. They encouraged me to swim through it, looking and touching it. Over a period of time I was helped to breathe slowly and relax. I've enjoyed some great times swimming with them and with Tina and Luke.

One of my favourite places I've swum at is Ansteys Cove. It is so peaceful and beautiful to be out there, simply exploring. Fishcombe Cove was another memorable swim as a large seal appeared, leading to a quick exit!

I am still nervous swimming in the sea, but it is probably one of the most amazing things I have done. I need to be in there more often to improve. I would thoroughly recommend anyone giving it a go, though ideally with a group of people who know and understand the dangers of the beautiful sea, like Happy Wild Swimming members.

Top: At Dawlish Airshow

Above: Luke with crab

Left: Me with Tina

The Mersey Mermaid

Julie Lloyd

I'm a 58 year old retired nurse. After retiring, I found open water swimming made me smile, especially as I was forced to give up a job I loved due to problems with my back. Even when I finish last in my swimming events, I always try to do so with a smile – so that's as good a reason as any to wear one on my hat.

My first ever swim was across the River Mersey!

Since then I've gone on to swim in rivers, lakes, lochs and big puddles.

Every year I complete one swim to raise funds for charity. This year I am swimming my 4 Nations Swim Tour in England, Ireland, Scotland & Wales. All the swims are in support of the new Royal Liverpool Hospital.

Of all the places I've swum in so far, one of my favourite swims is the River Severn Mile in Shrewsbury. It's a swim that has been going for less than 10 years and entrant numbers have been increasing year on year. Despite its short length of 1500m, it is not for some. The first 1000m are swimming with the current, but on turning at the English Bridge the final 500m are against the flow. I spent my first swim looking at the same flower on the river bank for quite some time! There is a nice friendly feel about this event and I look forward to swimming it again next year.

The River Liffey swim in Dublin was incredible. This iconic swim through the centre of Dublin is fast approaching its 100th anniversary. Predominantly a male only race, women have only been allowed entry since 1991 and I was proud to be able to take part. This is a compulsory non-wetsuit race which starts close to the gates of the Guinness factory and passes under 12 bridges, including the 50m wide O'Connell bridge. The race is run with gentleman first, then an hour later the ladies start. Each race starts with competitors and spectators singing Molly Malone. I can admit to having a lump in my throat. After passing under the green finish arch everyone goes through a decontamination shower provided by the Dublin Fire Brigade. I hope to return one day.

Also, I am proud to have completed the 'Coniston End to End' swim which is 5.25 miles, swimming the length of Coniston Water in the Lake District. It has been running for four years and this year there were over 700 swimmers set off in waves according to your mile swim time. In just a costume, hat, goggles and tow float I crossed the finish line in 3 hours 45 minutes. Not fast, not pretty, but I dragged myself over the finish with a smile. This swim was the longest event for me to date and I hope it will encourage more sponsors to help the new Royal Liverpool Hospital.

On my Dryrobe sleeve I have the words 'Jules The Mersey Mermaid'.

This year, I won a bronze medal for my age group (55-59) in the 1km British Championship at Chillswim Swim Gala. This festival of cold water swimming is held annually at the Low Wood Marina, in Lake Windermere, over 2 days. There are hundreds of competitors swimming 30m to 1000m, plus relay teams dressed in amazing costumes adding to the party atmosphere. Even the event commentator dresses as a polar bear.

So, if you enjoy cold water swimming, then this is an event not to be missed. If you like your martinis shaken not stirred then get your cocktail shaker ready for your post swim shivers and shakes!

Swimming outside always makes me smile and I think this photo sums up how I feel.

It was taken at the last swim of my 4 nations challenge swims, a 4 person relay of Loch Lomond.

We swam a total of 24 miles. Setting off in the dawning light, the water was relatively calm. Over the next 13 hours and 39 minutes we swam in wind, rain and sunshine. The water conditions changed from calm to choppy to calm again. During times when we struggled with the cold and wet conditions our mood would be lifted by the most beautiful rainbows. This was also a special day for me as it was my 58th birthday. Certainly one to remember!

I'm now looking to 2017 and hope to return to Scotland to have more smiles and more happy wild swims.

Photo opposite: A recent discrete meeting with a TV producer for a forthcoming programme in which I wore my Happy Cold Swimming cap. I can't say more at the time of writing but it was an exciting day.

126

Rekindled Love Of Swimming

Abby Fearon

I hadn't swum for 20 years and then someone mentioned the Dart 10k. "What a good idea," I thought, "I could do with a challenge". Before I knew what I was doing, I had entered. The only thing that stood between me and 10km of sheer joy was the small matter of some training!

I started out pootling behind my husband in his kayak from Stoke Gabriel, blissfully unaware of the seals that frequent that stretch of river. He would say things like "Why don't you just keep swimming?" I explained it was a lot harder than swimming in a pool. There was seaweed and other floating detritus, wind, chop and the thought of Sharks – yes even that far upstream!!! Then I discovered my husband had eaten all the emergency Jelly Babies whilst drifting about in the kayak, so I decided he was sacked as a training partner. That's when I found the Happy Wild Swimming group. I started off with leaking goggles and having to do a lot

of backstroke. I said it was because of the leaking goggles, but actually, looking down into 'the Blue' was quite terrifying. Unlike the River Dart, there actually could be sharks off the coast of Torquay – admittedly, the chances of meeting a bitey kind were slim, but the mind is a powerful thing! I have trialled a number of different coloured goggle lenses over that last couple of years, but I think it is rather the time spent in the water that has made me feel much more at ease.

With several visits to the Hindu Caves, swimming from Torquay harbour to Paignton harbour (and back) and a few more group swims in the River Dart, I had enough mileage under my belt to successfully complete the Dart 10k in quite a good time and thoroughly loved it! It had rekindled my love of swimming that had started as a teenager and now I needed a bigger challenge.

So I went off to Italy to swim the 14km Oceanman in Lago d'Orta. A lake swim with a beautiful scenic backdrop, which was amazing; fresh water (like the river), no sharks (like the river) and crystal clear (like the river ... no wait, that one's not true). After almost 5 hours of swimming I was completely exhausted and decided at that moment that people that swim the Channel are bonkers.

Since then, I have tried to fly the 'Happy Wild Swimming' flag wherever I have been. Although, there have been occasions where I have not made it

into the water. Whilst working in a hospital in Kenya I didn't fancy braving the wildlife to get in the waterways (mainly the microbial wildlife) so had to make do with wearing my Happy Wild Swimming cap horse riding instead!

This year has seen my 3rd entry into the Dart 10k and for the first time I entered the 'slow wave' doing a lot of breaststroke to 'enjoy the ride'. I saw a lot more of the scenery and wasn't half dead getting out at Dittisham. It's taken me 3 years to overcome my very competitive nature of 'going for the time' but I am finding it much better for the soul (and the shoulders!). I have learnt to overcome the illogical fear of sharks and the logical fear of seals and prefer to spend my swims catching crabs and enjoying the view!

However, I am still on the lookout for my next swimming experience.

I think Sweden could be calling next year!

To Whalsay Minus The Orcas

John William Simpson

On 29 July 2016, after much deliberation regarding the tides, 5 average swimmers - Julie Leask, Vanessa Irvine, Rhonda Sandison, Gibby Williamson and myself - set off from Stava Ness, mainland Shetland, to swim the 2.4 miles across to Whalsay, our home island, in order to raise £8000 for Cancer Research, a charity close to our hearts.

©Ivan Reid

We were supported by lots of small boats keeping a watchful eye on us as we swam and for what may be sharing the water with us. Around this time there was a lot of Orca (killer whale) activity in the Shetlands area. We were slightly apprehensive since in the days leading up to our planned swim a local swimmer had been charged by a bull Orca but it fortunately dipped underneath her at the last minute and left her to scramble ashore!

But, hey, it didn't hurt our charity campaign when that story was reported in the local newspaper. If anything it encouraged many more well wishers who welcomed us on our successful arrival at Sannik Beach, Whalsay.

We all agreed it was an awe inspiring experience crossing that tidal stretch of water. The sea was so clear and the atmosphere was great on reaching shore. I can highly recommend that swim to others.

Following a chat with Gary on Facebook, to make it memorable and fun, I bought the whole team 'happy caps'. He jokingly said the caps must have 'magical powers' as they had secured successes for all wearing them to swim the English Channel, Lake District and even from Ireland to Scotland! He was right too, as despite our swim being delayed for a few days, we completed it ... and minus the Orcas!

A true example of Happy Wild Swimming at its best - keep it up folks!

Photos by Ivan Reid

On My Head

As In My Heart

Lynda Wood

My first foray into open water was at 16 in the early 80s when I did the open water life guard course. To this day I remember the shock to the body of getting into an open lake without a wetsuit. I didn't do it for quite a while after that!

Now 30 years on, with the sport being enjoyed by so many, it is great to be part of a community of happy wild swimmers. I'm very happy to join in as wild swimming has made me happy and the caps really put the label on the experience of wearing on your head what you feel in your heart - cheesy but so true!

My 'happy caps' are well travelled and cause much amusement from onlookers.

In Sydney, Australia it was Golden Bondi Beach. In Portugal, the Golden Triangle.

An important swim for me happened in 2010. It was the motivation to get myself well after an illness that made me decide to challenge myself to a major event. The Byron Hellespont swim is an annual event swam in August when conditions are at their best. It's a tricky stretch of water, separating Europe and Asia. This one was the bicentennial anniversary of the poet Lord Byron's swim.

On 2nd May, we had our medical, did the acclimatisation swim and attended a briefing - lots of jellyfish (but not stingers!!!), strong chop expected and only 13 degrees. The then current record at 48 minutes; the shipping lane would be closed for 90 minutes after which we'd be pulled out. Also as the current was so strong the end point had been changed to give us a chance of getting in although it made it a longer crossing.

One hour and 27 minutes the legend Colin Hill finished first. The other 129 of us were well behind him. My one hour 53 minutes got me the age group Gold and also relief. In the end they kept the shipping lane open for 3 hours and still pulled out about 30 swimmers - organised chaos, but such an epic swim. To this day I believe that ignorance got me started and then I had to just finish. I still don't know quite how I did it, but it was one of the best experiences of my life and it was the start of swimming as much as I can in safe water.

The last meet up of pink-hatted swim buddies (aka 'The Portu-gals!) only took us along the coast to the nearest bar on day one and then a walk back. That's the danger of having a tow-float to keep your money in!

With my 50th coming up it's time to set the next challenge – so I'll be reading about all the Happy Wild Swimming experiences to make my mind up as to where to go next!

Most Important Swim Of My Life

Mike Speake

Three years ago after many years of competitive sport and an occupation of a postman and firefighter in Wales, I had to have a left knee replacement. What followed was six weeks of pain with a lack of movement and a lot of frustration.

During this time, I travelled down to Harcombe House, near Exeter, for specialist physiotherapy and rehabilitation with the Fire Fighters Charity. I was feeling very, very low at the possibility of not being able to do the things that I was used to.

So, whilst I sat in my room, I searched on Facebook for swimming opportunities around the area. Happily, I received an invite from Gary and Claire to go for a dip in Torquay. On arrival I was met by the friendliest couple in the world and made to feel so welcome.

I can honestly say that the swim that day in Torbay was probably the most important swim of my life so far.

Having changed and made our way to the beach, it was clear that Mother Nature had decided to test my recovery and stamina to its maximum. The afternoon sea was exceptionally lively, with waves crashing several feet up the nearby rocks as we entered.

However, comforted by their local knowledge and experience of this stretch of water, I was able to relax and make my decision to join Gary and Claire in the cauldron of white water. It was an incredible instant

exhilaration as my hands powered through the water. I was once again in action, enjoying the feeling of exercise and excitement that had taken me to successful Triathlon and swimming events, which I had doubted I may ever do again.

Throughout the swim it felt like a rollercoaster ride. One minute on a crest of a wave, the next plummeting into a trough, only to ride the next along to a new height. It was certainly fun trying to keep an eye on each other, but at no time did I feel we were in danger. Even when Gary laughed out loud at the realisation the waves were so high the mouth of a nearby cave was not visible, let alone accessible. I then realised that I can still do many of the things that I thought would be beyond me.

So to Gary and Claire I say, "Thank you both for being the perfect medicine!"

Sometime later, after feeling good enough to travel, I took a trip abroad. Where, under the heat of the Mediterranean sun, I proudly posed for fun in my Happy Wild Swimming cap, turned sideways for comical effect! (See my profile photo top left)

Happy Channel Relay Team

Tony Marshall

After swimming my epic 20 hour solo swim across the English Channel in 2015, I found myself thinking about the Channel again for both my own challenges as well as building a relay team.

The team would represent our local open water swimming club Chalkwell Redcaps and be raising sponsorship for Havens Children's Hospice. As I had worn my infamous yellow cap for my solo in July 2015 I would once again be flying the smiley flag for the Happy Wild Swimming community.

I put together a team to give other swimmers their first taste of the Channel with the backup of 5 extra swimmers for support and motivation. All of the team had open water swimming experience. One swimmer, Louise, had her solo already booked for 2017, but none apart from me had swum the Channel so the challenge was well and truly set. The team was made up of 3 girls and 3 guys giving a mixed balance of strength and experience with each swimmer bringing something different to the team. The team in relay swimming order were: (1) Justin Pitchford, (2) Alexandra Edge, (3) Mark Riley, (4) Louise Deering, (5) Fay Tuttlebury and (6) me, Tony Marshall. I was substituted in following the withdrawal of an injured swimmer from the original line-up.

Over the next few months everyone trained hard and kept each other up to date with training progress, unbeknown to the team I was hard at work in the background with the Happy Wild Swimming team of Claire and Gary organising team kit and it wasn't until the first team dinner that everyone was presented with their very own Happy Wild Swimming Channel Relay Dryrobe, swim caps and a team hoodie ... smiles all round.

It was then off to Dover to complete the 2 hour qualifying swim to ensure the team was fit and ready for the challenge ahead. The entire team swam together and motivated each other to reach the goal of passing the qualifier with the excitement of having the full team kit to warm up afterwards plus a few team photos too with the harbour and ferries as a backdrop.

A month passed and there were more frequent conversations between team members and a flurry of updates throughout the weeks as to who was doing what for their build up to the swim. The team thrived on banter and there was plenty of that flying around. With Justin's dislike of certain favoured footwear by Dover swimmers and Mark sailing across the Channel on his boat to take a look at what we were going to experience.

The swim slot was getting ever closer and the weather was not behaving itself in the Channel. A few swimmers had managed to get across but most had been delayed, so when our window finally opened on the 10th July 2016 we were hoping to get out early in the week. Every evening I would speak to Michael and Lance our pilot to plan the swim, the weather wasn't being kind. As the days passed there was frustration, questions asked and a feeling of impatience within the team, but I had absolute trust in our pilot and eventually we waited for 8 days before we got the final go ahead to swim. The whole team travelled to Dover on the 20th July 2016 to start the swim. We started later than expected due to Sea Satin coming back to Dover Marina a little later than scheduled with a solo swimmer on board who had finished her swim that morning.

With the team kit loaded, our Happy Wild Swimming flag flying high and Sea Satin refuelled, we set off. The weather couldn't have been better.

After days of high winds in the Channel, fog and generally bad weather, it had finally lifted giving an almost Mediterranean send off with the hottest day of the year so far, brilliant sunshine and flat water as we left the marina. We all lapped up the sunshine, praying it would last for our crossing. As we rounded the corner of the marina and headed along the coast to Abbots Cliff, Justin dutifully got ready to swim and at 10:41 am dressed in his union flag budgie smuggler trunks and a pink Happy Wild Swimming cap he jumped into the water and swam ashore to officially start our swim.

It was a strong start from Justin who took us out of the pull of the White Cliffs of Dover coastline.

Alex took over an hour in and swam strongly throughout her hour, handing over to Mark who pulled us out into the Channel with strength and speed.

Louise was next up and took us through the first shipping lane, getting very close to a passing container ship who just wanted to get a closer look at a happy Channel swimmer cap, so left it very late to change course. Once she was through the shipping lane Fay took over for her first hour slot. Somehow she managed to miss any encounters with jellyfish while taking us into the

separation zone, where I took over and swam through a variety of nasties before handing back to Justin to start off round 2.

We were having a great time in the Channel. Everyone supporting each swimmer in the water, happy Dryrobes protecting us all from getting cold and plenty of food to keep us all going, some of which didn't look too appetising, more like pet food.

Round 2 of swimming took us into the night where Fay swam from daylight through to darkness. We could see the French coastline, the wind was picking up and the swell was a little choppier than our opening swims, but we all forged ahead and made good time.

Lights on and talk soon turned to landing in France.

I kept the team focused on their swims.

As we saw the coastline getting ever closer it turned to swimmer number 4 Louise, to swim us into the French coastline and onto the sandy beach North of Wissant at 03:03 am French

time with the whole team right behind her, everyone walking up the final part together to share the team experience of having landed on French sand.

The team had successfully made it across the Channel in a time of 15 hours and 24 minutes. We stopped for a small but well earned celebration on the beach before swimming back to the boat, getting warm and dry and caught up on much needed sleep back on the trip back to Dover.

Job Done!

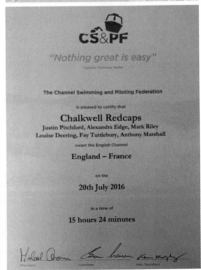

CS&PF

"Nothing great is easy"

The Channel Swimming and Piloting Federation

is pleased to certify that

Chalkwell Redcaps

Justin Pitchford, Alexandra Edge, Mark Riley
Louise Deering, Fay Tuttlebury, Anthony Marshall

swam the English Channel

England – France

on the

20th July 2016

in a time of

15 hours 24 minutes

Grab The Moment

Mitch Tonks

I feel totally at one with myself when in the sea. That first refreshing sensation as you dive under is so cleansing, that cold feeling around the head is a wonderful feeling.

What I love most about the sea is that two days are never exactly the same. I recall a swim with Gary and Claire off Preston Sands, Torbay. They wouldn't know, but it was one of my finest early morning swims.

The light was golden, the sea flat and clear and the sun warm on the face.

Previously, I hadn't done much swimming in the sea, so it was all new to me, but I enjoyed swimming in company and learning the ropes to wild swimming. I came back a few days later to enjoy more of the same, but the wind had gone east, the water now cloudy and the sun not out.

It made me realise more and more that you just have to grab the moment and get in the sea when conditions are right because they won't wait until you are ready.

Leave it and you will miss out!

Definitely In Her Name

Ocean by Nicki Brown

My daughter, Ocean, is a typical lively, friendly, happy 10 year old girl, who lives on Jersey, the largest of the Channel Islands, surrounded by the sea. So, it is imperative that you learn to swim from a young age. She started swimming with Sally Minty-Gravett MBE in the swimming pool, early 2015. As soon as Ocean started her lessons, Sally noticed a potential in her and she quickly moved up the swimming levels.

After encouragement from Sally to join the Jersey Long Distance Swimming Club, she started to swim in the sea in May 2015. Since that time, Ocean has not looked back. She has gone from strength to strength, with the help and guidance from Sally.

Ocean was awarded the Girls Junior Endeavour Trophy in November 2015 for Jersey Long Distance Swimming Club and she has already won her first accolade "Flambard Trophy" for most improved swimmer this year, 2016.

In the summer she completed another challenge. An organised event with Jersey Hospice Care and National Trust of Jersey, where you had to swim in 30 bays during the 30 days of July, whilst raising money via sponsorship for these two very worthwhile charities. Ocean raised £650.

Ocean embarked on her challenge with enthusiasm and excitement,

romoting Sea Safety with Rescue Services   St Aubin Fort with Sea Cadet Leader John

accompanied by so many people on her swims. We tried to swim with a different person every day, but it wasn't always easy! Sally was her main stay and she swam with her in several places.

Amongst the 30 bays, 2 stood out. At La Rocque on the high tide at 7 am, when Ocean swam across the bay with Sally and 2 friends, then around the pier, finishing by jumping off the pier and all completed in time for school. The other was swimming from Flicquet to La Coupe bay. On this particular day, the sea was like glass, the weather was stunning sunshine and you could have been anywhere in the world, yet we were in our gorgeous island of Jersey.

Ocean's ultimate goals are to swim round Jersey as part of a relay team, swim round Jersey solo and swim the English Channel - at the moment she is too young to do this. It won't be too long though. With her stamina and determination, before we know it, she will embark on all these adventures. We will continue to encourage and support Ocean as far as she wants to go in her challenges. For now, the love of the Ocean, is definitely in her name!

Bucket List Day In Shetland

Ryan Leith

Shetland is a group of islands lying to the north of the Scottish mainland between the Atlantic Ocean and the North Sea. Due to the North Atlantic Current bringing warm water north from the tropics, the climate is remarkably temperate considering Shetland shares a latitude of 60 degrees north with southern Greenland, Alaska and the Kamchatka Peninsula in Russia.

The sea temperature varies between 5 and 12 degrees Celsius so swimming is possible at any time of year with a good wetsuit! With hundreds of beaches, headlands and inlets (known locally as voes) you can always find a sheltered location, whatever direction the relentless wind is blowing from.

The Atlantic swell battering a volcanic headland, known as Eshaness, for millennia, has created one of Shetland's most spectacular coastal features a huge cave at Calders Geo, which has been explored by so few people it is yet to be named. Having free dived the cave a few years ago, I recently lead a group of local swimmers to witness the cavernous interior of the cave for themselves. After an hour's drive north from Lerwick we arrived at the Eshaness Lighthouse, a very popular location for visitors to take photos of the spectacular coastline. Only a very small number of them have any idea of the vast, empty space beneath them as they stroll along the coast.

After a short walk along the 200 foot high cliffs, we climbed down an ancient lava flow to our entry point for the swim. The weather conditions were ideal, with light winds and only a slight swell running in from the Atlantic. Numerous small fish hovered over the kelp forest as we swam around a headland towards the cave, before the seabed disappeared from view into the deep.

We entered the cave by the smaller of the two western entrances, a long wide tunnel leading us into the dark interior of the cave and our first view of the underground cavern, the largest in the UK. Soft corals grow on the walls and seals cruise between the massive basalt blocks that have fallen

from the roof of the cave, during the fury of countless Shetland winters.

Sunbeams light the low, southern entrance of the cave as we swim through, out into the open space of Calders Geo. After taking photos I lead the group back into the darkness along the eastern wall of the cave, disturbing a colony of kittiwakes who voice their disapproval. Fishing buoys are jammed in cracks high above our heads, a reminder of the power that created this subterranean world.

All too soon it is time to head back to the shore. We pass out through the main entrance to the cave, which is so big it could easily swallow a modern fishing trawler. Conditions allow us to swim between some offshore stacks, through aerated water and foam, back towards our tongue of lava, the only safe exit point along this section of coast.

Coffee and home bakes are very welcome after over an hour in the sea. All agree that our swim has been a memorable one ... a bucket list day!

Photo above: Exploring inside Knab Cave during another Shetland swim

Swimming
Side By Side

Danny Bunn

Open water swimming attracts an eclectic bunch. There's the hippy-dippy mermaids who need to feel 'at one' with nature, ice paddlers who live for the (mind) numbing experience of the 'polar endorphin crackle' or testosterone soaked types with more computing power on their forearm than NASA had available for the moon landings and everyone in between.

Chris and I are a couple of has-been (never-was) pool swimmers who got bored of the black line so we took it outside - in rubber. We are also lazy with respect to wetsuit cleaning, so we soon ditched those too. Ah – the freedom from hosing down neoprene after every swim and then leaving it to dry, hung-up in the bathroom, to scare our unsuspecting partners!

Then, we got bored of swimming in circles in lakes where small things lived, so progressed to salt-water where unseen, bigger things lived. We completed a few races and then we got bored with those. We wanted something different. Something we'd never done before. Something we could start without the knowledge that we could finish it.

We found our challenge in the 7 mile Walton Pier to Clacton Pier sea swim. A race course that was popular in the 70s (pre-health and safety, risk assessment and child protection legislation) but had not been swum for decades. We checked in with a few old hands from 30 years ago. We sought advice from local race organisers, the coastguard and others we felt we could help. Some of the advice was useful and some of the comments we received were encouraging.

By now we knew the date, the tide and the likely conditions. We also knew we were fudging the safety issue somewhat. No matter, we should be ok. Driving to the coast our mantra was "if it's not 100% ok, we're calling it off". Peeking over the sea wall we saw a flattish sea. The wind was fairly low too. The swim was on.

7 miles in wetsuits and hi-viz tow floats with some energy bars and drinks. The coastguard knew we were going in and we had a spectator on the beach keeping a watchful eye. Our plan was to stop after the first 400m to check wetsuits, goggles etc and then stop when needed. At the first break it was smiles all round. The sea wasn't cold, the sun was shining and goggles and wetsuits were feeling good. Only 6 ¾ miles to go! The first couple of miles were pretty easy. Swimming side by side we soon got into our rhythm on the slack part of the tide.

This was swimming at its best. A couple of mates doing what they loved, side by side. No egos were involved, we were swimming at a fair clip, but the point of the swim was the swim; not the time or who touched first – just enjoy the moment and the waves. After an hour we stopped and floated around. Drinks were taken, Mars bars eaten, a brief chat and a wave to the shore which was 400 metres away. We could see the coast curved quite a lot on the next session; we had to swim round a corner and then it should be a straight run to the finish.

As we rounded the corner, several things immediately became clear. The tide was now picking up to our advantage, we were in deeper (colder) water and we were a lot further from the shore than we thought - over half a mile now. The plan was to keep swimming towards the finish and the tide was to push us towards the beach. That was the plan. The reality was somewhat different.

Shortly after, a boat started coming towards us. Not a little, inquisitive pleasure craft. No, a massive thing, full of rocks with a dumper truck in the back that was helping to rebuild the sea defences. We couldn't go beach side of it, so we decided to go out further (¾ mile) to go around it. Deeper and colder but it felt safer. Mini-crisis over we carried on and now had the incentive of being able to just see the finish line in the distance. Pushing on we were now 2 hours into the swim. Fatigue was creeping up on us and the constant bobbing wasn't great for 2 landlubbers. The highlight of the swim was having a seagull hover about 6 feet above us for at least 10 minutes. Every breath it was there. It didn't crap on us luckily.

Another stop - the last one we hoped. By now the salt and the motion combined to predictable results and I saw my Mars bars and energy drinks for the second time that day. I'd had enough now. "Not far now" was the new mantra. "About 1km left, almost a warm-up" was another. My personal favourite was "Let's get this thing done so we never have to do it again".

Over the next 20 minutes Chris and I battled in. We were tiring and the tide wasn't particularly helpful. A couple of jet skiers came over to check we were ok. A thumbs up from all parties and they were gone.

There is a point in every hard swim, be it a challenging pool set, a set distance or a set time when you know, just know, that you will finish. We were at that point now. Shoulders were hurting, stomachs were cramping and each stroke was a real effort but the probability of finishing was moving towards us. We just had to keep turning the arms over and we would get there – we both knew it and upped the effort (if not the pace) to bring this swim to a close.

Finally, after 3 hours and 15 minutes we reached the end. Absolutely exhausted, we touched the pier and slowly paddled to the shore that thankfully was now only 200 metres away. Chris was quiet behind me, an emotional one, that boy. He seemed to 'have something in his eye' whilst I just sat there trying to take in the achievement. We could never repeat the experience on this swim; it was the first time we attempted and completed it. We would come back a year later to swim it again with friends and they had the same sense of achievement as we had, but for me and Chris – 'the pioneers' – completing a swim that we didn't know we could finish was an amazing experience.

Without doubt this is the swim that we had most connection with. The planning, the protocols and the execution made it something special; a happy swim indeed.

Planes, Trains & Automobiles

Claire Bunker-Fellingham

Swimming provides moments of thrilling sights and fun-filled pleasure ... and not always to do with things in the water!

In the few years since Gary and I took up the hobby of swimming outdoors, we've encountered the usual swimming companions of other water users like kayakers, SUPs, yachts, jet-skiers, added to seabirds, fish, seaweeds, jellyfish and seals. We've enjoyed a variety of scenery along coastlines, coves, riverbanks, inside sea caves and amazing ever-changing colours in the water and sky.

Mix into it many wonderful times with friends as well as strangers in and out of the water and swimming has kindly provided a lovely mix of nice memories.

Some of the more unusual ones for us include unexpected

joys of swimming out at sea while the Red Arrows display team fly overhead, walking underneath a steam train to get to a sea swim and enjoying a taxi ride over fields to the group campsite on the bonnet of a swim buddy's Landrover – great times with friends enjoying the simple pleasure of swimming outside – what we call Happy Wild Swimming.

"Vrolijke Wilde Badmutsen"

Hugo Sinke

Perhaps I'm one of the few happy owners of a Happy Wild Swimming cap that is not so much into wild swimming. There, I said it - that will probably make you think, "Why do I own a crispy white Happy Wild Swimming cap?" Here's the story:

Allow me to introduce myself. Hugo Sinke (1971), married, no kids and I live in the Netherlands. In my free time I like to do social activities and sports. One of my passions is to do (full) triathlons, hence the need to swim once in a while. I am a Navy Officer in the Royal Netherlands Navy.

In 2013, I stepped on board HNLMS Tromp as the Executive Officer and we conducted an extensive workup program. The final six weeks of workup are conducted in the Plymouth Exercise areas. This is where the Royal Navy's, Flag Officer Sea Training (FOST), trains both UK and foreign ships. On a daily basis, so called seariders from FOST, embark the ships to conduct the training. Some seariders are responsible for complete departments, others will focus on individuals. This is where I met my British colleague Dave who became my personal coach – or shadow - over a six week timeframe. During the six weeks, we had plenty of time to discuss work and non-work related issues and that's where we discussed my passion for sports in general and triathlons in particular. On the day of the final inspection (the last day of training), Dave was so kind to present me with a 'happy cap' and told me the story behind the Happy Wild Swimming community.

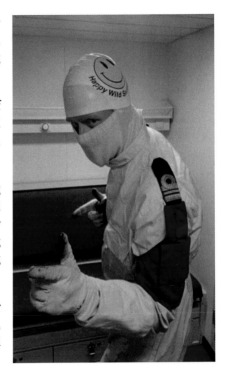

Have I worn my cap? As a matter of fact I have. Not so much to do wild swims but generally to swim in swimming pools.

I've also been taking my cap along on my travels (both business and private) as I like to assist the Happy Wild Swimming group in spreading the smiles around the globe adding to the group map.

Places I've taken my cap so far include: The Netherlands, France, Saint Martin, Curacao, Aruba and Bali (Indonesia).

I'm sure there are more places to come soon!

Note: "Vrolijke Wilde Badmutsen" is Dutch for Happy Wild Swimming.

Photos: Below left pool training; Below right, Seminyak, Bali.

I Want To Swim Out There

Sally Bird

OK, so this is how it all began for me.

Back in 2008, I was diagnosed with chronic obstructive pulmonary disease, sometimes unable to walk from one room to the other. Then, following a year on steroids, my immune system was affected by fungal spores. Two days later, I broke my back coming off my bike, 4 weeks before my 60th birthday! For over 4 months I spent 24/7 in a brace and was scared to ride my mountain bike again which was something I loved.

I read an article about walking along the sea and how you can absorb various nutrients which are good for your immune system. So I started doing this. Then, in April 2013, one morning at 5.30 am, (I even know the date), I stared out to a misty sea and thought, "I want to swim out there!"

In the sea I can be me. Go any direction, go under or just float and look at the sky. There is no wrong way to get along in the sea. Ultimately, I am in control of what I am doing.

It has given me so much zest for life. Meeting so many others who enjoy exactly the same thing and being involved in many different swims.

My most memorable swim has to be swimming when we had snow in February 2015 - what fun and excitement for an old biddy!

What swimmer doesn't like laughing and occasionally eating cake?
So, yes, life is good!

Flying To France World Record

Mark Johansen

Sunday 9th August 2015, is a day that will stay with me forever. It was approaching 10pm and I was on a boat being buffeted around in the English Channel just North West of Calais.

The Fly to France team - Kevin Blick, Robert Fisher, Sam Mould, Rob Ouldcott, Boris Mavra and myself - were attempting to be the first relay to cross the English Channel swimming butterfly.

It had been a day of two halves. The first saw flat seas and sunshine, the second windy, rough and teeming with jellyfish.

The Guinness book of records had allowed us 20 hours in which to set the record, so it was starting to look touch and go whether we would succeed, indeed we weren't even sure we were going to make land at all and finish the swim.

Butterfly is a slow stroke for swimming long distances, so the tide had carried us much further East up the Channel and we were rapidly approaching Calais. This meant we were facing the prospect of having to abort the swim. There is a relatively narrow channel that shipping uses to get in and out of the Port of Calais and it's a busy one, with huge ferries coming in and out every 15 minutes. We were now approaching the edge of this channel and had been swimming an hour each for 17 hours as Sam entered the water for the third time.

Once a swimmer passes east of the harbour wall at Calais, it signals game over as the land then drops away and makes it impossible to finish a swim as the tides sweep you up towards the North Sea.

Understandably the port authorities aren't keen on swimmers crossing the channel in to the port, but they do grudgingly allow it, as long as you can make it across safely between the ferries.

The 500m dash across the ferry lane might not sound far, but remember we were swimming butterfly, we were tired, each of us had already swum 3 hours. Also, it was dark, cold and conditions were very rough, plus huge ferries were looming up in front of us.

Five of us on the team were experienced Channel swimmers having completed at least one solo crossing each. Sam on the other hand, was on her first Channel swim and had only taken up butterfly a few months previously. It was unlikely she could make it across between the ships, so our Pilot, Neil Streeter, made an important tactical decision. He turned the boat west so that Sam was now swimming straight into the tide, theory being that if she could just hold position enough to ensure we didn't drift any closer to the port, the next swimmer could then sprint us across the channel to safety.

I think Sam sensed something wasn't quite right as she kept looking across at the boat as if seeking reassurance. All we could do was yell encouragement and urge her to keep going. At hour 18, Sam finished her final hour and it was now time for our fastest swimmer, team captain Kevin Blick to get in and take us across, but he had been incredibly sick throughout the entire day and had suffered the worst of the jellyfish swarms. He was physically spent and looked awful as he jumped in to start his fourth hour. If he couldn't make it we were finished.

Sam got out of the water. We helped her dry off and get dressed, got her warm and then told her what she's just done for the team - you can imagine her response!

We had 2 hours left to set the record, the shore seemed so close, but the Channel wasn't done with us yet. There was another enormous ferry heading to port, so, like Sam, Kevin also had to swim into the tide and hold our position for 15 minutes until it passed. Once it had gone the Calais authorities told us we had one chance to get through or we would have to abort.

Neil turned the boat south again, Kevin took his cue and somehow found the energy to sprint across and go on to finish his final hour. It was a huge relief as Kevin was replaced by Rob who swam the final 15 minutes to finish the swim just west of Calais at 12.05am.

The swim had taken us 19 hours 15 minutes and as Rob (accompanied by Boris for safety) walked up the beach, we knew we had set a new World Record. It was a special moment for us all.

We'd witnessed some amazing moments on the crossing, including seeing a whale pass behind the boat. We'd all faced individual challenges during the crossing and shared the tension of what became a real race to the finish, but most of all we all knew that we'd created a special bond between the six of us. It's a friendship to cherish forever and one that will endure to form the basis of more adventures.

It all seems a far cry from being taken by my dad to our local Victorian baths for my first swimming lessons 45 years ago. I remember the smell of the chlorine, the glass atrium ceiling dripping with condensation and stained by mould. There were changing cubicles along the side of the pool where my dad would rub my hair dry with a scratchy old towel. I can't say I took to it like the proverbial duck, but I always enjoyed the vending machine hot chocolate afterwards.

That pool is now a function room used for weddings and other celebrations. I wonder if any of the revellers there now stop to think about how many adventures like mine were spawned in the pool that was once under their feet? I reckon very few.

My Favourite Wild Swim

Simon Griffiths

I always find it difficult to answer any question about favourites. The idea of having a favourite colour or number seems quite bizarre in fact. Why should I like one more than the other?

With wild swims, it's possibly even harder to pick one I like more than any other. It's also not so easy to define exactly what we mean by wild swimming. I'm sure it's one of those things where everyone thinks they know what it is but if asked to put it into words would come up with something unique. For me, it's non-competitive swimming in a natural environment.

There should be an element of exploration and the experience is more important than the destination.

I would therefore exclude swimming laps in a commercial venue – not because I don't like doing that (I do) but because it's too regulated.

As for wetsuits, I take a pragmatic approach. I love the feeling of cool water against my skin and feel more comfortable swimming without one but I hate getting too cold. I've been in hospital once with hypothermia and I don't want to do that again. I will therefore happily put on a wetsuit if the swim is lengthy or will involve a lot of hanging around or chatting.

The best wild swims need the right combination of place, conditions and people. A spot might be ideal one day and dangerous the next. A good example of this is Stranglers Beach on the North Cornish coast near Crackington Haven.

The whole experience of visiting Stranglers deserves to be savoured as to get there you need to descend a narrow path down the cliff from where you have spectacular views across the bay. The beach is always quiet, even on a hot bank holiday, and has a mixture of sand and pebbles (which change shape as you move along the coast). However, it is often not suitable for doing much in the water except for surfing (if you're sufficiently skilled) or jumping the incoming waves. It is rough, visibility is low because of churned up sand, there are hidden rocks, occasional rip currents, no lifeguards and no mobile phone signal to call for help if needed. On the other hand, one day this summer, the sea was perfectly calm with visibility extending to several metres under the water. I enjoyed a delightful swim along the coast with my sister with views back onto the fractured cliffs above and shimmering fish below.

This definitely counts as one of my favourites.

Some of the best wild swimming I've done was in the South of France with my family. Ribaute on the Orbieu stands out. It has a large pool for

swimming, water falls to scramble up and down and, for the brave or foolhardy, a high bridge for leaping from. The water is cool but you can quickly warm up by stretching out on the rounded limestone rocks and soaking up the sun. It's also an incredibly scenic spot.

Finally, although it's too far from where I live to visit as often as I'd like, the English Lake District ticks all the boxes for wild swimming: hundreds of spots to choose from, amazing backdrop and (mostly) freedom to swim where you like. This summer when I went (but not every summer) the water was also surprisingly warm.

Simon Griffiths - founder and publisher of H2Open Magazine

***

H2Open Magazine is inspirational reading for anyone who loves swimming outdoors whether you're looking for the best spots for some fun wild swimming or training for a long distance challenge.

Published six times a year, you can start with a trial subscription for as little as £8.70 for 3 issues. Find out more: www.h2openmagazine.com

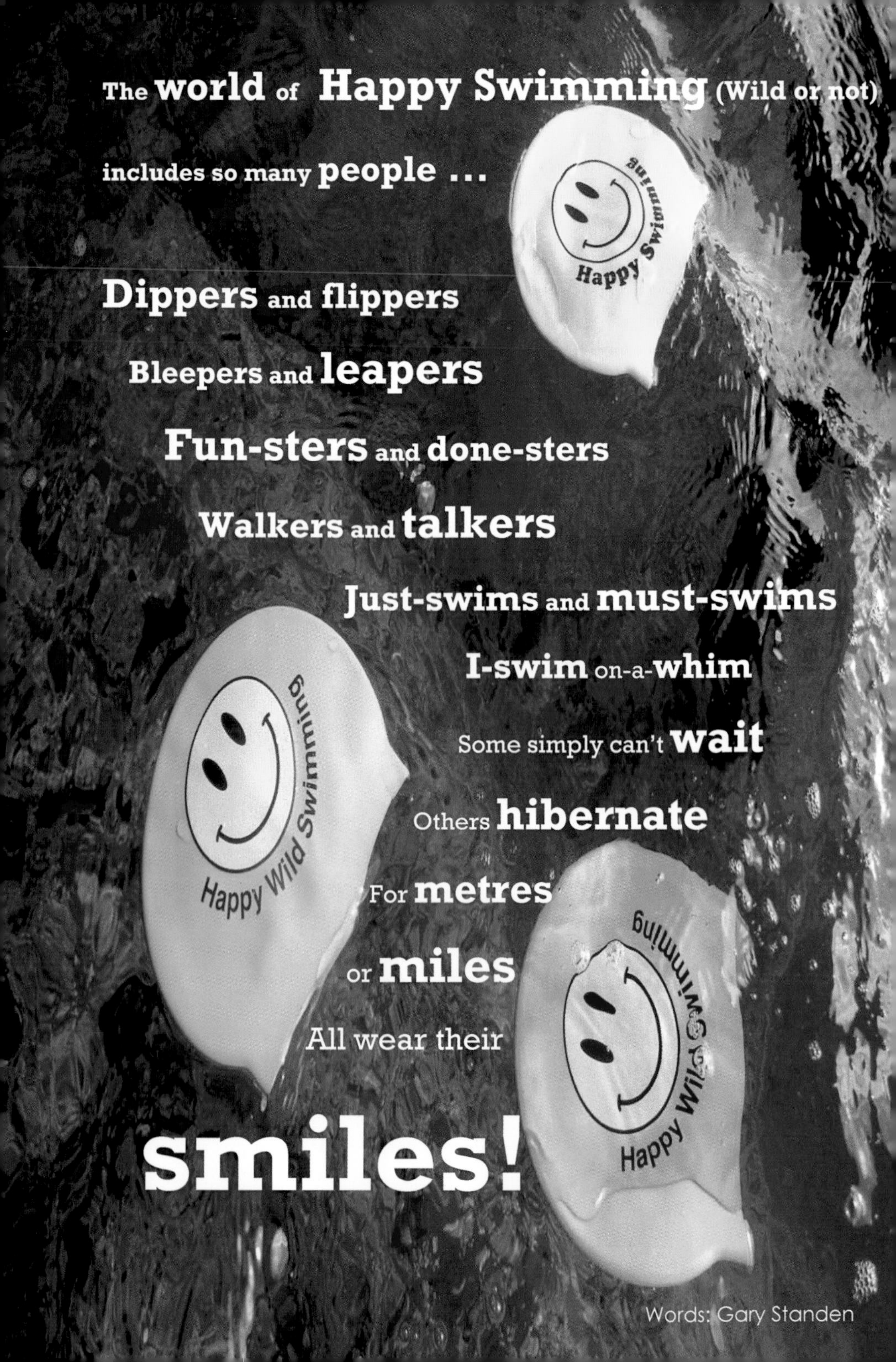
The world of Happy Swimming (Wild or not)
includes so many people ...
Dippers and flippers
Bleepers and leapers
Fun-sters and done-sters
Walkers and talkers
Just-swims and must-swims
I-swim on-a-whim
Some simply can't wait
Others hibernate
For metres
or miles
All wear their
smiles!
Happy Swimming
Happy Wild Swimming
Happy Wild Swimming
Words: Gary Standen

Happy Smiles Are Medals

Gary Standen

I've enjoyed achieving results but I believe true success is being happy.

As a quiet teenager, I grew in confidence through my sporting successes. I started to thrive on the winning feeling, both as an individual and in a team. I competed in many sports, though none were in the water, being appointed captain of several different team sports while at grammar school. I also enjoyed being the fastest sprinter at 100 and 200 metres for two years running and my most pleasing success was being signed-up by my local professional football team, Brighton & Hove Albion, just before I turned 15 years old. At such a young age, I was privileged to experience almost 4 years of professional standard training, daily fitness regimes and competitive, driven focus for match day perfection. (Clearly I was holding the team back though, as a few years after I'd chosen to leave in favour of a career in finance and playing semi-professional, they famously played Manchester United in the FA Cup Final!).

Very fond memories I cherish to this day. They provided an appreciation of what dedication and determination can give anyone, whatever their background or circumstances. Winning brought huge smiles and feelings of incredible satisfaction. However, the sting was that anything less than a perfect result brought negative emotions, often lasting many days.

My letter requesting a football trial was never replied to. I attended the local trials uninvited, simply tagging along to watch a friend with my ever-present kit bag slung over my shoulder. When the coach requested all attendees to gather into groups per playing position, I just joined in. I don't know why I did that, I was still a very shy 14 year old lad who would normally wait to be asked rather than push in. The year before I hadn't even been a regular in the school football team, yet at that moment something compelled me to 'get involved'. I stripped off and lined-up, while my friend did similarly in a different group unaware of my action. The coach looked at his clipboard and asked me, "Who are you? You're not on my invited list. I need to chat with your parents to ask why you're here". I explained I was alone, simply doing what made me happy. He walked off to consult with the newly appointed manager, ex-England player Alan Mullery, who looking over from a distance was seen to nod and the rest is my teenage history. The trials progressed; I kept being retained for next stages throughout the day and made the final cut of just 6 players from over 3000 on trial that day. A few days later, the coach visited my parents' home for me to sign my contract. (Unfortunately, my friend didn't make it past the first cut and upset, had left with his mum soon after. Knowing how hopeful he had been, his disappointment was a stark reminder of the downside to not achieving ambition).

Now here's the point - as great as all the euphoric feelings are of sporting successes and ego-boosting personal achievements, I can honestly say I've found more meaningful happiness when 'in the moment' of a simple swim. I only learned to sea swim in recent years and now in my 55th year of 'still learning' how to live well, one lesson I have learned is that it's never too late to find what makes you happy. In the open water I feel a success of my own creation. Whether I swim head down or float to relax, with a group or alone, I always enjoy it. That is success.

Life is a journey during which we strive to be happy as often as we can. No competition needed. Being happy in what we do is the win we can all achieve. Personal ambitions are very important, but better than any winner's medal for me has been finding something that naturally makes me smile and being able to help others find theirs too.

Since creating and sharing our 'Happy Caps', the reward for me (and Claire) is seeing images of others smiling - individual and team successes without any medals. Happy smiles are medals well worth collecting!

Photo opposite above: Claire Bunker-Fellingham
Photo opposite below: Miles Redhead

See Where It Takes You

Fay Brereton

Why do I swim outside in the sea, lakes and rivers? Why not?

I was brought up on a peninsular in the north west of England, surrounded by the sea and rivers on three sides. Adventures lead me to explore the lands of Snowdonia where I found some delicious mountain lakes, cool, crisp and clear to dip my weary feet in. I wondered, how deep are the lakes that nestled here under Wales highest peak and how much could I see under water? The next moment - in I went, knowing I had some miles to walk in the bright sun before I found my car again at Pen y pass. I embraced the opportunity to answer my own curiosity with the lakes invitation to cool down. The first thing that I expected of course was the cold water against my skin. How cold in reality was evident in my facial expression upon the water reaching my chest. A feeling of the cold penetrating into my soul was exhilarating and something historically, I may not have been alone in experiencing. Exiting the lake and continuing my journey down the miners track, I wondered if those who had shared that experience were the tough Welsh miners after a hard days graft. With that thought I smiled.

Finding myself some time later resident in Devon, the sea was close once again. A friend had asked if I would like to swim the great north swim in Windermere. Well, I have mountain biked Claife Heights with views across the lake, I have canoed across the water with school as a child and I have often walked the fells surrounding the large expanse of cold, clear, crisp water. So full circle I thought, brilliant idea and why not?

So up and down in an enclosed chlorine filled trough called the local baths, early mornings before work, became my training routine towards coping with the required 2 miles distance. As I was now into surfing I knew I'd appreciate the benefits of a neoprene layer, so I purchased my first wetsuit to swim in. Those Welsh miners were tough - I'm not Welsh, nor a miner.

The day came and we swam really well, totally enjoying the exhilaration that 2 miles in open water brings. No lanes, no lines to follow and no chlorine. The fells were beautiful seen from the water early in June sunlight and I remembered all the adventures I'd had biking and walking those lands. Sharing the moment with my friend, in the water feeling the environment around me, completed the picture of Windermere - a very special place.

I enjoy thinking about why I love to swim and where that comes from. Just being by the sea is a big draw for me and it is important to know it is there. Like a comfort blanket!

My advice to anyone would be to explore and feel your environment at that very moment. Even the watery ones may bring nice surprises. Here in Devon, there are red cliffs against blue sea with secret little caves and beaches waiting to be found. Just dip your toe in and see where it takes you. I guarantee a smile.

Cheers At The Fairy Pools

Melanie McAinsh

I'm very proud of my happy hat.

Back in 2014 I purchased my visible Happy Wild Swimming cap. It had a great first week including visits to Threipmuir Reservoir near Balerno in the Pentland Hills, the River Braan, the River Inver and to meet new friends at the Wild Ones, Portobello Beach, Edinburgh.

A year later, I was at the Fairy Pools on the Isle of Skye where some of these photos were taken. Previous attempts were foiled by howling gales so I was delighted to finally get to swim here. However, it wasn't straightforward.

I realised that I couldn't climb down the now eroded drop. I was just about to give up, exasperated and a bit emotional, when I was fortunately rescued by a local Skye mountain guide, Ian. With an impromptu quick climbing lesson provided, he kindly accompanied me down the wet, rocky descent and back up. Trust me, it looked much bigger looking down!

The Gabbro Rock archway is located between these delightful pools and I wanted to include it while I was here. However, when I dived under it, a massive cheer went up. I hadn't noticed the busloads of tourists who had gathered and were watching me. Not the most solitude filled swim, though one of my most memorable.

One thing to bear in mind if visiting is that going under Gabbro Rock was harder than I thought it would be, due to wearing my wetsuit. My advice, as I will do myself next time I visit, is to do so on a hot summer's day and swim it in swimmers (cossie) only!

The Original
Water Baby

Sandy Johnson Carosi

If you asked them, my parents would say I could swim before I could walk. Mom was a part time swim teacher in college and I was their experimental baby for 'Learn to Swim'.

I wasn't aware of people who couldn't swim at an early age. I thought it was natural that everyone could swim. So I guess you could say I was the original water baby.

Once, at a company family picnic of my dad's, when I wasn't quite two years old, I jumped off the diving board. The company president jumped in after me, not knowing I could swim. My parents tell me I was really annoyed at him. My mom still has a newspaper article with a picture of me jumping into the pool at age two.

Back in those days my dad never dreamed that he'd be my support kayaker for many long distance sea swims.

174

I have proudly worn my Happy Swimming and Happy Wild Swimming caps for several major swims. Twice for the 12.5 mile swim around Key West and once out to Alligator Lighthouse and back 9 miles.

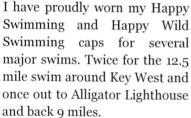

When it comes to swimming caps I hoard them, along with swim suits, similar to runners hoarding their shoes before they get changed to the next best model. So as soon as I saw the fun happy caps were available, albeit having to wait for them to arrive to USA from England, I just had to have some ... and later on some more.

Here in The Garden State of New Jersey, USA, I wear them every day and people recognise me for doing this.

Keep swimming everyone!

The Feeling
Of Elation

Jennie Harwood

At the ridiculous age of 52, I got badgered into getting into Lake 32 in the Cotswold Water Park, during the cold month of March. My open water swimming adventures had begun.

In September 2015, I reaped the reward for all my efforts to train as I swam the Dart 10k event, completing it in a time of 3 hours 4 minutes.

Less than a year later, in July 2016, I swam in the Mediterranean Sea from Gozo to Malta in 3 hours 9 minutes - a truly amazing swim, but dreadful organisation and no support boats. The Italians and Maltese did well as they knew the route, the rest of us got lost. There were no markers, no helpers - in fact it was quite dangerous. There were general boats and luckily they were quite helpful, but this was without doubt one of the worst 3 hours of my life! My friend who was swimming alongside me was seasick and just wanted to get out, so to have had a support boat to get out onto would have been very handy.

A month after that, in August 2016, along with 17 of my swim chums from Lake 32, we swam the Thames Marathon. The course was 14km, swimming along the River Thames from Henley to Marlow. This is a tough challenging swim and much more difficult than the River Dart.

I started training as soon as the lake water warmed up. As part of my training, I swam 5 lots of at least 4 hour swims, which were only just about enough. The Dart was a lovely scenic swim, assisted by a helpful current. In comparison, Henley had none of this. I didn't even notice a tide at all. In addition, the Thames has many locks breaking up the river, so we had to keep climbing out. I kept thinking to myself each time I climbed a ladder in the respective locks, that this is more like an army assault course. The locks split the swimming into sections of 4km, 6km, 1.5km and 2.5km of actual swimming, interrupted by scrambling in and out of the water, which made for an unusual swim, to say the least. Also, I found myself swimming most of it solo, which I didn't mind. But it's much harder to do that over a long distance. I just kept focused on swimming towards the tow float in front of me. When I swam past some people in the medium wave, that was fun and it spurred me on. I managed to sprint the last 2 stages, as I was absolutely determined to finish in 4 hours 30 minutes. Unfortunately, I got held up a couple of times and ended up finishing in 4 hours 40 minutes, to then see my chums standing at the top of yet more steps which I needed to climb to exit the Thames.

I did enjoy it and I would do it again. But next time I would build into my training at least 3 swims of 5 hours to be better prepared.

To undertake marathon swimming is hard. It is mind over matter and it can be dull. However, the feeling of elation you get from completing the distance is just amazing.

In 2017, I'm thinking I'd like to swim the length of Lake Windermere, a distance of 10.5 miles. The training will involve more long swims, requiring me to endure yet more pain. To me, it's all worth it when I receive the finish medals and the friends I get to meet along the way.

In between events I've made time to pop down to South Devon to enjoy several social swims with the local Happy Wild Swimming group. These have included swimming through sea caves, under a natural Arch and along some stunning coastline.

In addition, I've returned to the River Dart to swim with them a few times, most recently a shorter section of around 4km up river to the riverside pub for lunch. That was an entertaining swim as not only were my companions good fun, but first there was the revelation in the water that a seal was stalking us and then Gary suggested we swim to the riverbank for a photo with some cows. He was aware my own local group is the Cotswolds Open Water Swimmers – the COWS – a photo opportunity too good to miss.

Can't Get Any Better Than That

Lisa North

As a child I swam with a local swimming club until I went to secondary school and then the running and hockey took over. All my summers were spent down the beach at Poole in Dorset and I loved being near or in the sea the whole day no matter what the weather.

I took up open water swimming about 20 years ago when I got a running injury. Like many other people who got injured at that time I ended up taking part in triathlon so several times a week I would meet other triathletes and we would swim a 2km route parallel to the shore. Every time we would do the same thing without deviation from May until September when it was deemed too cold and we would head back in the pool for our triathlon swimming training.

Then, in 2013, I discovered proper open water swimming when I ditched the wetsuit. I started swimming 'skins' (in just a costume, without a wetsuit) with the encouragement and support of other local like minded people instead of the triathletes I had previously swum with.

Before a short time I was swimming for several hours at a time and signed up for an English Channel relay. Not just any relay, in fact a four person double relay with the legend that is Marc Newman.

This gave me a taster of things to come. Three years later, I've completed the hardest physical challenge I have ever undertaken. This was a 2 person 2 way English Channel crossing and was billed as a 'World First'. As one half of the team called 'Gangsta Grannies', I swam 2 hours at a time with my partner Ali Budynkiewicz (one of the original ladies that encouraged me to ditch the wetsuit) taking over while I rested. We took 31 hours and 28 minutes.

This swim was made very special, as my oldest grandchild, 8 year old Bradley, came with me to Dover and was on the beach at Samphire Hoe where I started. It was fantastic that I could see him, give him a hug and a kiss as I embarked on the biggest swimming challenge I will probably ever do. When I had to dig deep to keep going, I just thought of my happy, smiley boy, all the swims we've shared together and all those waiting to be done. That was brilliant and it can't get any better than that.

Other memorable swims include, swimming around Brownsea Island a total of 6 times now and being one of a handful of people who successfully swam the Dart 10 miles challenge (the longer swim of the more frequently swam Dart 10k event). In addition, I have completed several ironman triathlons, as well as running/walking 3 marathons over 3 days and cycling several 100+ miles events. I am not really interested in being fast or first across the finish line. I look for the adventure, the challenge, pushing myself to achieve a goal and training hard to get there.

I hope that I am a role model for other women, mothers and grandmothers, as well as my own children and grandchildren.

Bradley has watched me undertake various swim, run and cycle events. So when I challenged him to target his own challenges, he whole heartedly agreed. Since the summer of him being 5 years old, we have named a swimming challenge he will do during the school holidays.

We started swimming out about 20 metres to the buoy and back. Later on we swam underneath Durdle Door. When he was 7 years old, he swam 500 metres in the sea at our local beach. This year, aged 8, he swam through Durdle Door and round to Man O' War bay, part of the Jurassic coastline.

Next year, we are planning Lulworth Cove to Stair Hole. Doing these challenges with my grandson has given me an enormous amount of pleasure and I am so proud of Bradley. It's not about him following in my footsteps, it's more that he is doing what he wants to do and getting out into the real world, experiencing life. Surely this is what all kids should be doing so they can tell their friends and children about their adventures.

I worry about exposing him to unnecessary risks and of course I do not want anything bad to happen to him, but equally I hope these challenges will set him up for adulthood where he can make his own decisions and live life to the full. We have created our own swimming adventures making all my Channel swims and races worthwhile.

I am so lucky Bradley is my grandson.

He is my main inspiration and keeps me ...

"Swimming with smiles"

Seeking Out Swimmers

Sammy Seal

I swim daily. Sometimes, I swim far out to sea and other times close to shore. I enjoy the freedom of the sea and love eating fish. Some days, I like nothing more than to seek out and follow swimmers. More often than not, I creep up behind them while they are in full stroke and simply follow behind, about a metre away from their feet. It's a good game, as rarely do the swimmers know I'm even there!

On occasions, I make sure they are aware of my presence by sticking my head out of the water, waiting until I'm spotted and then darting back under to re-emerge in a slightly different place. To my amusement this can create havoc among my audience. Particularly, amusing is their reaction if I bob about a bit nearby and then disappear under for quite awhile, leaving them guessing as to where I have gone and when will I return? Relatives of mine report having similar pleasure in various locations, but my preferred home is Brixham, Devon.

One day, a few years ago, I was swimming back from a late morning venture into deeper water, when I spotted two swimmers dressed to look like me, making their way steadily along the coast. They had got in just before the headland known as Berry Head and were swimming towards Breakwater Beach. At the halfway point, they had passed Shoalstone Pool a sea-water filled lido and were treading water to take photos of the coastline from in the water. This was an opportunity too good to miss!

It was a gorgeous day. A perfectly clear sky, met the deep blue calm sea. The lido was busy with plenty of onlookers around to enjoy my antics. I took sight of the happy swimmers from 30 metres away and headed towards them, breaking the sea surface as I did, to ensure the spectators at the lido would notice me. They pointed and called out to me, but I was fully focused on my mischievous intent to catch up with the swimmers. It turns out they were called Gary and Claire. They had recently become sea confident and this swim as a couple was their first off shore, away from any group swim. To them it was quite a significant mini adventure to share. So it was only fair I added some extra drama to make it a fully memorable experience.

I switched into stealth mode. I went under and swam the rest of the distance hidden from view. This was going to be fun. They were totally unaware I was in the water, let alone underneath their dangling legs!

Utilising all my experience of past approaches, I suddenly popped up behind Claire. The look on Gary's face was brilliant. An instant mix of fright and wonderment, his expression seemingly confused as to whether he should call out or stare in admiration at my magnificent huge appearance. I always ensure my eyes are as big and wide as possible, the size of a man's fists, with my long whiskers glistening against my silky grey-black coat and I like to give a brief flash of my long teeth (although I try not to breathe out as I haven't yet learned to use toothpaste and my breath is quite foul). As the only large male in this location, I have my reputation to live up to. Too often the smaller females or juveniles are mistaken for me, but you only need to see me once to know which one I am. I'm the big boy!

So, as I burst into the view of Gary, it was understandable that he looked spooked. However, he quickly gathered his composure and made a simple request to Claire, whose back was to me. "Give me the camera" he uttered. Apparently, the tone of his request said far more to Claire. She immediately interpreted his few words, as "Oh no! The huge seal has appeared right next to you and is about to eat you! Let me get it on film."

Claire's beaming smile left in a blink and was replaced by the strangest of expressions. Clearly, she was unsure whether he was playing a prank on her, so I thought I'd help explain the situation to her. I swiftly ducked down, swam underneath her, to be able to give Gary's calf a quick tug, just enough to pull him down a few inches, before reappearing immediately behind him. Now I was in full view of Claire, she no longer needed to question if I was present or not and whether I was a lot bigger than Gary. She could instantly see for herself that I was both these things!

She didn't stay to chat, though. Instead, she evolved into the cartoon Taz the Tasmanian Devil. Her eyes tried to leave her head on stalks, her mouth opened wider than her dentist has ever seen and her arms attempted to detach themselves from her body as she swung them around in her state of panic. She was brilliant! She gave me the best reaction I've ever had to a sudden appearance. It made my day!

She made it even more entertaining when she turned to bolt off towards shore in a freestyle speed worthy of an Olympian, her camera dangling beneath her still fastened to her waist strap. Gary looked at me and I looked at him, both of us in disbelief at what we had just witnessed. Then, without a word (but I understood what the game was to be) Gary also swam away. He grappled with the camera in one hand, preventing me taking it in my teeth, while swimming with his other hand to keep up with the speedy Claire. Oh, it was fun! Just a few minutes, but hilarious!

They were swimming erratically on top, while I swam gracefully behind them, briefly popping underneath each of them, before gliding slightly menacingly alongside them. The moment passed quickly as soon they had scrambled over some rocks and onto the nearby beach. There they sat looking back at me. I gave a little smile as I saw the relief come over their faces and then each laughed out loud. Only then were they aware we had had a sizeable audience from both the lido and the day tourists on the beach. As a last gesture, Gary did point the camera towards me for a quick snap from shore, an attempt to obtain a photographic memento, but I was already dunking under the water, preparing to swim off. As grateful as I was for their companionship, I knew there were more unsuspecting swimmers to be sought out. As we seals say, when one encounter ends and another is due; "There are always plenty more swimmers in the sea!"

Eye Opening
And Exhilarating

Deborah Herridge

I've been Happy Wild Swimming now for three wonderful years, which have been some of the best years of my life and I've never smiled so much! It all started with a little dip in the Solent, having been inspired by the London 2012 Olympics and Paralympics to get fit. Outdoor swimming has made me look at water in a different light, usually with the question, "Can I swim in that?"

I have ventured far and wide, to the beautiful waters off Devon and Cornwall, to the crystal clear turquoise waters of the stunning Isle of Mull, where I have swum with many seals and where it is possible to see whales, basking sharks, otters and porpoises, to the dark and mysterious waters of Loch Lomond. The world is now my swimming oyster, to be discovered and swam.

I'm not ashamed to say that swimming has become a bit of an addiction, but a good one.

It is an addiction that makes you healthier, happier and makes you see things from a different view point. Seeing the land that you know from the water is both eye opening and exhilarating, as is night swimming, which I adore, a wonderful experience for all the senses.

It's not all just for fun and smiles, although a smile always accompanies a swim. I also love to push my body and the distances I can do, as well as

enjoying the feel of the water and the great outdoors with all it encompasses. So far in the past few years I've completed a 7 mile swim diagonally across the very busy 'Solent' on the south coast of England. Last year I completed an inaugural two-way swim of 14 miles from Hill Head Sailing Club to Ryde and back again, an epic adventure on the high seas, having to swim the last few hours in a Force 6, but best of all, through all of this and people's very generous spirit, we have raised 10k for charity. I am on a mission for my next big swim and to raise even more for worthy causes that are close to my heart.

Sometime between 28th August and the 4th September 2017 I will set off from Dover and swim the 21 miles across the English Channel to France.

The Channel is famously unpredictable and one of the busiest shipping routes in the world. I will have a pilot boat alongside me guiding my way and once I start the swim, I will not be allowed to touch the boat or a person until I step on French sand/rocks. I'm told that more people have climbed Mount Everest than swam the English Channel.

The likelihood is that the swim will cover many more miles with the tides pushing me sideways when it changes every 6 hours. Most swimmers paths are an 'S' shape because of this. The swim will take around 14 - 16 hours or more depending on the weather and conditions on the day. As always, I just swim in my swimsuit, cap and goggles without any assistance from the thermal qualities and buoyancy of a wetsuit, since these are not allowed under the official 'Channel Rules'.

My training this year took a real blow back in the spring when I was diagnosed with pneumonia meaning I couldn't do anything for 3 months. I literally spent the time sitting and reading, having no energy at all. One after affect of it was chronic fatigue, but I gradually  built up my fitness, starting with a ten minute swim at the end of June and improving steadily through the summer. I'm behind on my original schedule, but on the positive side it has all been very good mental training for the Channel. The frustrations I've felt at not being able to do anything and the patience I've learnt throughout this awful time. If my pilot tells me I've missed the tide and will have to swim for another 5 hours I will simply put my head down, get on with the job and hope I reach France. My determination will not waiver.

www.justgiving.com/teams/DeborahsEnglishChannelSwim

To The Rock In Suits Then Skins

Simon Parkin

The hottest day of the year so far. So hot that even the air-conditioning has given up for the day as I drive down to South Devon after work. I swelter down endless country lanes until I round a corner and see it – an arch in the middle of the bay like a noble statue in the middle of a town square – Thurlestone Rock.

I meet up with friends from the Happy Wild Swimming group with the aim of swimming out to this tiny tidal island. I've been so hot all day that I wonder about swimming without my wetsuit on. A quick reccy at the water's edge, feeling the colder than expected temperature of the sea, soon dissuades me. "Sod that!" I go and get my wetsuit from the car.

It's been a while since I've swum in the sea and I'm nervous. I don't know what I'm scared of exactly but the rock seems a long way away. The sea

feels gargantuan and intimidating at eye level as we enter the water. It's cold and smells of rotten seaweed. I get my head under the surface for a second and loose tendrils of seaweed appear in front of my goggles making me jump and splutter. Clouds begin to encroach on the sky and darken the water. Through the murk I see a shadow of a shoal of fish. They're making way for us as we swim towards the rock. The sight fills me with delight and dread in equal parts.

As I acclimatize to the cold sea, I swim with my head down in the water, surveying the crevices in the rock beneath me for creatures. I stop for a break and all of a sudden the rock is right there in front of me. Now I can see the arch properly and it lies perpendicular to the beach. It's a grand sight towering above us like a jagged slice of cathedral dome. We swim through and play on the slightly submerged rocks. Someone spots a compass jellyfish beneath them, its dirty brown crossed dome sinks into the seaweed as I float over, its tentacles sprawling menacingly. Then a blue jellyfish, neon and otherworldly. As the slight current moves the seaweed and me at the same time I have the disorientating illusion of enormous boulders on the sea floor washing around in the waves.

A group of teenagers in bikinis and shorts have swum out to the rock and start bombing each other, shouting and laughing. I feel like a wimp.

In a wave of melancholia I wonder why I've driven for two hours in a hot car just to swim to a rock. Do I like swimming as much as I convince myself? Is it worth it? Really? A gush of cold water floods down my back.

I take my time swimming back, not wanting to be in a hot car again. Chatting to a swimming friend as we scull backwards to the shore, the rock towering over us with translucent clouds behind it is backlit by the now setting sun.

In the shallows Claire, Ruth and Gary take their wetsuits off in the water to save the usual squeaky wrestling match on the beach. Gary suggests I do too and throws them in a pile of neoprene on the shoreline and we dive back into the water with just swimming costumes on. It's a fresh jolt and we whoop with the shock. It feels good.

Then, without discussion, without foresight, we swim back towards the rock. I swim with a fast pace to try and warm up, grabbing lungfuls of air as I power along, shoveling sea water behind me. The sun finally breaks free and lights up the sea beneath me as it rushes past, seaweed fronds billowing. My body feels free of restriction and I stretch my arms to the horizon with each stroke, the cold tickling my ribs, my muscles taut. I look up and my friends are doing the same, heads down, racing to the rock. Even quicker than before, we're back in the shadows of Thurlestone Rock. I swim away from the others, full of confidence now and too cold to stop and chat anyway. As I round the rock the low sun appears from behind it and blasts through the water in front of me, showing up its deep range of aqua hues.

I look around me and take it all in: the hotel on the headland bathing in the last light of the day; the crowds on the beach slowly dispersing, sticky with suncream; the multi-layered clouds above me and framed through the arch; Burgh Island in the distance with its magnificent Art Deco hotel. I'm buzzing with the light and the cold and the view.

On the drive home, Book at Bedtime on the radio, I know it was worth it. Swims always are.

Solent Dream To Rod Mania

Mandy Parent

Hi there. I hope you enjoy reading my swimming escapades.

In January 2014, I had the burning desire to swim the Solent – that very large expanse of water which stretches between Portsmouth and the Isle of Wight. I sat on the beach and I wondered and pondered. Then one day I decided to enquire how to cross this bit of sea I was so intrigued about. I found that the West Wight Sports Centre on the Isle of Wight did a charity swim on the shorter, much choppier crossing near the Needles, between Hurst Castle and Colwell Bay. I was too late to sign up (no change there then), so I was added to the reserve list. I didn't think too much about it and swam a few lengths in the pool here and there, only about 8 in total to be honest and I certainly didn't practise in the sea.

One Wednesday in the middle of May, I got an email asking if I still wanted a place as someone had dropped out due to illness/injury. OMG! It's really happening. Next thing, I had signed up and paid my money. I had just 3 days before I needed to go over to West Wight Sports Centre for a swim test – just a mere 100 lengths to test my timing and pair me up with a similar swimmer. EEEEEKKKKK!!!!

I didn't have a wetsuit, but managed to acquire one via the local diving club. It was a diving wetsuit, which I assumed was absolutely fine. I swam 80 lengths the following day (I work better under pressure), then caught the ferry over and completed the 100 length test. Oh yeah, bring it on. My dream was becoming a reality.

So now, the training really had to begin. After one or two scary sea swims on my own (which I now know you should never do), I joined the

Portsmouth Triathlete swimmers. I knew they swam in the sea twice a week and it would be good to swim in a crowd for training. I kept my distance as these uber fit people would never understand what I was trying to do and I certainly didn't run any more or ride a bike, apart from to Waitrose. So, I kept in the background, turned up, swam, went home.

On Sunday 6 July 2014, I swam the Solent, in my diving wetsuit!

With renewed confidence, I arrived at the Tri Club beach huts HQ the following week brimming with pride at my achievement. I turned up in my diving wetsuit. "You can't swim in that" one said. Another said the same and so it went on. My reply was, "I just did, thanks ... I swam the Solent actually". I never knew how uncool I was by not having 'the right wetsuit', but, hey, I did it and that's the main thing.

As time went on I got to know more people and chatted to some of the crazies there. I bought a new tri-wetsuit which was like a different world swimming in that compared to my previous one.

The laughs began and in 2015 I started to enjoy the club and the friends I'd made more and more. Happy and crazy people like Debbie Pentland, Marie-Adele Hargreaves and my "Tri Wife" Louise Miller (we did our first triathlon together in 2015 – she had never swum in the sea before then).

I completed my first triathlon in June 2015, in Portsmouth and was so, so proud. I had been even more nervous doing that than my Solent swim!

In August 2015, I turned 50 and a very good friend of mine, knowing I was supposed to go and see my idol Rod Stewart in Las Vegas, which never materialised, he bought me a cardboard cut out of Rod for my birthday instead – and so the Rod madness began! He was taken on a tour of the Isle of Wight and a Park Run where he was held for me by my good friend Eric de Greef.

Rod became a regular visitor to the Portsmouth Tri Club beach hut HQ. He has featured at many of our sunrise swims at 6am – unofficial ones for the craziest of our Tri bunch and even appeared on Smiler, the Rod Stewart Fan Club page, as part of an article ... and of course wearing his Happy Wild Swimming Cap!

KEEEEEEP SWIMMING!!!!!!!

Swimming Is Like Air To Me

Sandra Lavender

In 1992 at the age of 29, I sustained a compound fracture of my femur and a fracture of my skull. I was subsequently unconscious for a week; I had been run over by a car after falling off my bike.

I was on my way to college where I was training to be a secondary school PE Teacher. I had decided to take this up as a mature student so my accident changed my life when I was only 29 years old. I stayed in hospital for 3 months and then underwent a long rehabilitation. One of the exercises I had to do was in a hydrotherapy pool, but as I had little control over my body I had to wear a life jacket.

At that point in time I had been a swimming teacher for around 8 years. I had never been a competitive swimmer, but I was a strong one. At college, I was truly privileged to have trained under and have as my personal tutor in my final year, the late Helen Elkington, an immensely experienced and renowned coach. I hadn't learnt to swim until the age of 18, but I had this love of water, in fact, a real passion. In water I felt free and no one could see my wobbly bits. No one could see my inflexibility; I didn't have to 'look the part'. So, now in this hydro pool I should be smiling from ear to ear. However, I was terrified, simply terrified. I thought every minute I was going to drown. The strong swimmer that I had been was now totally reliant of others. This experience I can now look back on and say that it helped me in so many ways. It made me truly empathetic as a swimming teacher, especially for those terrified adult learners. It also strengthened my passion for swimming.

With my husband's job we get to travel quite a bit and we spent some time in Cyprus where I took up sea swimming. Now I ask you, who wouldn't in that beautiful crystal clear blue Mediterranean Sea?! Eventually we had to come back to the UK, where a friend and I decided to do the Great Swims Challenge completing 4 of the 5 Great Swims in 2014 - the final one, in London, being cancelled the day before! However, you can't just come from the 'toasty'

Med and swim happily in the UK lakes and rivers, so I had to find somewhere to train. I found the most lovely group of swimmers, in the Cotswolds, called COWS (Cotswold Open Water Swimmers). It was with them that I found I could truly begin to call myself an OWS, as we took dips in winter with the lake water temperatures of 1C–4C! Swimming out in the open in all of the British seasons was just an absolute delight, each having its highlight. Swimming in a lake at night too was another first back in the UK. It's the utter feeling of freedom I suppose, like sky diving, though that is something I will never do.

As I write, I am in China and I would not recommend swimming in most of their rivers or lakes. Finding open water that you can actually swim in has been difficult, but I have swum in the Ming Tomb reservoir (below) and in the summertime during the week I swim in an open air pool. Where next? Who knows? But I can say that once you've swum outside, I mean properly swum outside, there's no indoor pool that can satisfy!

This is only a brief snippet of my swimming experience but to sum up my water passion I quote my mother-in-law a few months after my accident: "I realise now that swimming for you is like air ... you need it to survive!"

Around Goat Island Swim

Paul Fowler

I have had the good fortune to swim in a number of places throughout the UK and Europe. One of my favourite locations to swim in has to be Sivota, Greece and in particular the 2.2km 'Around Goat Island Swim'.

Staying at the hillside retreat 'Neilson Beach Club', each morning you draw the curtains back to a glorious view across still warm water to a tree lined almond shaped 'Goat Island'. Access to the Island is very simple as there is a spit that can be walked across at no more than thigh depth.

On the island itself is a water sports centre for wind surfers, stand up paddle boarders and Laser sailors. Swimming is generally restricted between the hotel and the island in a buoyed area. However, once a week, guests are invited to take part in an event 'The Around Goat Island Swim'.

This swim is easily navigable with supporting kayakers and boats on hand. A highlight is swimming through a glorious rock arch at the rear of the island. It feels much lower than it actually is and so most swimmers handle this stretch with great caution.

After swimming the Island in 2012 I was fortunate to return for a week with my wife in 2013. The week was to combine both holiday and swim training ready for a 25 mile endurance swim later in the summer. Each day, with permission of the resort manager I was able to swim laps of the island solo, basically until hungry! I would come in, eat and then return for a further session after an hour or so.

Swimming solo gave the swim such an amazing different edge. It wasn't just sighting for myself without a guide, but the self-responsibility for safety and welfare once out of sight. During the first few days of swimming I remember that I didn't dare swim through the arch once. I elected instead to swim an additional 500m around the stacks at the far pinnacle of the island. I had enough to contend with; rise and fall of the swell for one and these swims seemed rougher than when I swam in 2012.

As the days passed I realised that I would achieve my planned target of 80km for the week around this 2.2km track. By the Thursday I was ready for a big day and managed 10 loops split into two sessions clocking a total of 23.5km (allowing for drift/poor sighting) over the 22km (10 x 2.2km) I was happy and classed this a very good day of training.

As Friday came around I prepped for my pre breakfast swim and my wife reminded me that Friday was 'The' Goat Island Swim Event itself. Now as this felt like my home turf I figured I really ought to have a really good go at it. There was a triathlete camp in situ for the week and some of the Scottish attendees were ex university swimmers – so I knew it would be fast and I was ready for some interval training and company!

After swimming two laps before breakfast I got myself to the start line for a 10 am race start. Most swimmers were there for fun but the tri camp swimmers seemed rather concerned that I had lined up beside them without a wetsuit. Friendly chaps but they just seemed a little confused.

As the hooter sounded I wished them a great race and set off. Unfortunately the lead kayaker took a bit of a poor line, which with the experience of the week behind me I knew to be wrong. So within 1km I was clear of the pack and found myself in a great

place out front. It was good to be swimming with others and to be honest I had wanted the company for longer as I had been swimming by myself all week after all - but it was not to be.

I returned to the sailing club, (Start/Finish line) 26 minutes after I had started. It was confirmed that I was indeed the first home. After light refreshment and waiting to congratulate my fellow swimmers on completing their lap, a few people elected to swim another, which I was happy to join in with. Upon our return my wife informed me that as I had won the event we had been invited to a presentation dinner.

That evening we went along had a great dinner and had a little wine of course. At the presentation itself I received my winner's certificate and hearty congratulations. The chap presenting then started to regale that although I might be fast, there had been a hotel guest here who had been repeatedly swimming the island "round and around and around" all week! To which I simply had to say "well he sounds nuts, but if you find him he can gladly have my certificate, thank you very much". Then I retired for an early night and a flight home the next day.

Contact me for friendly help and advice, coaching and open water events in the East Midlands via www.onehundredpercentswimming.co.uk

The International 4SeaAbles

Deborah (Dory) Johns

I am not sure what possessed me but it seemed a really good idea at the time - a way to combine my 60th birthday with fundraising for MS Australia - a perfect combination.

I approached Chloe McCardel, a world champion marathon swimmer who has now swum across the English Channel 18 times, about joining one of her relay teams. The fact that I had only been swimming for a short while, after a more than 40 year break, seemed not to be relevant to me. I didn't think that having never swum in open water before would be an obstacle either - suffice to say that it has been a torrid learning curve.

Chloe accepted my application and my training commenced. Always a pool swimmer I found open water swimming challenging. So challenging that I had panic attacks - my first ever. They were terrifying. I would get in the open water and all my air would be sucked out of my body. My arms and legs felt like they were jelly. I knew, intellectually, that I could do the distance. I couldn't work out why it was happening. Worrying about it started to dominate my life. I tried all sorts of things but nothing seemed to help. I would start swimming and have to stop to try and get air in or revert to breaststroke. It was certainly not going to be the way to swim the English Channel. One night my son and I were talking about his acting and I asked how come he didn't get stage fright. He said it was because he was a character on stage. He suggested I pretend to be a 'character' when I swam and so my swimming persona of 'Dory' was born. On my next open water swim as 'Dory' the familiar panic set in - and then stopped!

I qualified for the English Channel relay on 24 April 2016 in Tasmania by doing a 2 hour swim in water that was 14.1 degrees Celsius (you must swim for two hours in water that is 15.5 degrees Celsius or below in order to qualify to swim in an official English Channel crossing).

Chloe included me in a four-person international relay team, comprising Kerry Yonushonis from the USA, Xavier Tordoir from Belgium and Leonie Webb from Australia. We called ourselves the 4SeaAbles.

From left: Kerry, Xavier, Leonie, Dory, Chloe (coach), Dan (support crew USA)

Things didn't go quite as planned with my preparation. I tore the meniscus in my left knee in October last year. The orthopaedic surgeon suggested surgery. I didn't think I could spare the couple of months off training. We tried the less invasive platelet rich plasma (PRP) treatment where they take your blood, extract the platelets and inject the concentration in the affected area. The injections, right into the joint, were hideous. The treatments helped, but I couldn't kick properly, so I put more effort into my arm stroke resulting in a biceps tendon tear. More physio! I felt like I was living at the physiotherapist's. I worried that I was going to let the team down, but I didn't at any stage think about 'throwing in the towel'. Why, I don't know.

Here I was, nearly 60, fat, had just quit smoking and body seemingly falling apart, yet I knew deep down that somehow it would work out. I sought help with my stroke and spent three months making changes to my arm stroke technique, breathing and body rotation, to swim more smoothly. It was hard to make those changes but bit by bit things started to improve. By the time I arrived in Dover I was swimming strongly, not as fast as Chloe had wanted me to, but a comfortable 3 km an hour. I was still worried - now it was about how I would get on and off the boat. I hate heights and wondered if my knee would let me get up the ladder. At least Chloe had been very firm in making sure we had good anti-seasickness meds that we had tried well before the swim.

So the big day arrived and Xavier started our relay off. It was pitch black. As I stared into the darkness I was glad it wasn't me out there in the water. Kerry went in next. She had swum the Catalina Channel a few weeks before. She swam beautifully - even a problem with her goggles didn't faze her. Leonie, the other Aussie and the only team member I had met before we all arrived in Dover, was third in. She loved every minute of her swim.

I was fourth in. I looked down at the water that seemed so far below me. I remember shaking from fear of the jump - but I jumped in from the back of the boat when told to. As I went into the water I took in a lungful of diesel fumes. I think I swore. The hour-long swim felt like it was going on forever. I told myself, "Just keep swimming!"

I saw the sunrise. A board got held up on the boat saying I had another half-hour to swim. Seriously? I started counting strokes. I told myself to enjoy the experience. I tried, but that was hard to do when it felt like I was never going to finish. Finally, my hour was up. I clambered up the ladder at the back of the boat, taking in another lungful of diesel. I just sat on the boat. I wasn't hungry and didn't feel particularly tired. I drank some water and watched Xavier swimming - and so it went.

We were making great time. I went in for my third swim. No matter what I did I couldn't get away from the diesel fumes. I also noticed we seemed to be going in a big arc. Something wasn't quite right but I didn't know what. I remember thinking to myself, "Surely we aren't going in a circle?" The boat kept going in a curve. I kept following it. I got back on board. The French coast was really close but we had hit the 'washing machine'. We were told there was a really strong likelihood we would not land.

It took us nearly two hours to cover those last two miles. Xavier and then Kerry battled through awful turbulence. Finally, Kerry landed in France, at Cap Gris Nez, on the slipway of the restaurant La Sirène, very fitting as sirène means mermaid in French.

We were all allowed to swim in behind her, where we got our French pebble, said hello to those on shore and then swam back to the boat.

We had taken 13 hours 44 minutes and had swum 50.6 kilometres (over 31 miles). I can say that each of us put our heart and soul into every hour we were in the water.

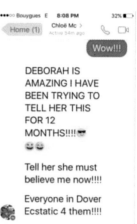

When we got back on the boat, my phone was out of charge, so I asked Dan, who was our support crew, to send a message to our coach Chloe from me telling her, "I didn't stop. I kept on swimming!" Dan looked at me quizzically but sent the message anyway.

Chloe wrote back (see text message opposite)

I burst into tears on reading her reply.

Of all the memories from that day, the most prominent for me is the journey of over two hours it took for the boat to get us back to Dover. As I looked back at France I couldn't believe how far we had swum that day.

Photo below: Team celebrating with Dan leaving France to return to Dover

I thought about a day less than 4 years ago when a friend dragged me back into the pool kicking and screaming, after more than 40 years out of the water. It was now less than two years since I had first tried open water swimming and a week to my 60th birthday. How my life had changed!

We were all pretty quiet on the trip back. Soft conversations as we each thought about what we had achieved as a team. I remember looking back at the French shore in the distance and thinking about Chloe's triple crossing last year. I wondered how on earth did she have the strength to swim to France, only to turn around to swim back, then turn around at Dover and swim back to France yet again? Then I remembered Chloe telling me that the thing about swimming the English Channel is that after the first time you will either decide that is it, you have done it and you don't want to do it again, or you will fall in love with it and want to go back and do it again and again. Now I understand what she was talking about. I am not sure I am in love with the English Channel but I can certainly hear her siren call luring me back to swim across her again.

The swim itself is a blur and sometime later still has a dreamlike feel to it.

Photo: Adding 4SeaAbles to the swimmers wall at White Horse Inn, Dover

Devon To St. Kitts And Back Again

Lin Cram

In 2015, I was camping in a field overlooking Burgh Island in Devon when a friendly couple, Claire and Gary, said hello and commented that they had just swum around the island. Earlier that day, I had swum the Pub-to-Pub swim with Ghislaine who said she was swimming down the river from Aveton to Bantham with the group. After confirming I was confident of the distance (some 6km) and that Ghislaine had kindly given me a happy cap to wear, I was welcomed to join in and 24 hours later I had swum my first swim, swimming with smiles. It really was a fun swim and made my trip more memorable. All too soon though, the swimmers were heading off to their respective homes around England and I was on route to my home in Wales, hoping to stay in touch with them.

Months passed and I swam with my local swimming friends in Wales – by the way, the Welsh for Happy Wild Swimming is 'Nofio Gwyllt Hapus'

Left Top: Mynydd Carningli overlooking the river Nyfer

Left: Meeting at the start of the annual river swim with the Happy Wild Swimming group in Devon

I took a trip to St. Kitts with my happy cap where I swam the 2.5 miles channel crossing from Nevis to St. Kitts (Oualie beach to Cockleshell Bay) – in the pouring rain! A strong current from the south clashed with a westerly wind. Waves were breaking over my head, troughs to one side, breakers to the other. I am not terribly brave, so I shut my eyes when breathing in and opened them underwater to watch the various turtles (green, hawksbill and loggerheads) and the rays (southern stingray and spotted eagle ray), taking my mind off the waves. This crossing is also a race and the conditions we were not always as we experienced, this year the swim was re-routed to a coastal swim, due to these winds. I was swimming with Valerie, who lives on Nevis, following her feet. Even she felt seasick by the end. Not a typical Caribbean day at all. In fact a jolly hard swim.

I returned just in time to find out the group I'd met the year before were about to return to the same place for the current year's annual swims and camping weekend - another chance to enjoy time with them so I made my plans and not too long after I was once again in the river swimming along with smiles all around me – more happy memories.

Another swim I've enjoyed is a fabulous fresh water location. I'm not sure I'm keen to share this spot, but I know many other people know about it already. This photo doesn't do it justice or show how quiet it was ... at

least it was when I was there. It is Blue Lake, near Dolgellau, North Wales - a truly beautiful spot, with fantastically blue water in a former slate quarry.

Worth a look if you're visiting the area and can find it.

Getting In
Grandad's Way

Jock Bagnall

This is a short recollection of the time I and my friend Danny, were swimming across to Horse Island, situated off the coast at Ardrossan, a town on the North Ayrshire coast in south-western Scotland.

We considered this stretch of water to be our local swimming pool, to the rest of the world it's called the Firth of Clyde. However, the area is a natural barrier where many ships have run aground or sunk. Nowadays, the island still possesses the same dangers but is now a nature reserve run by the RSPB with special protection status because water fowl use the beaches as breeding, nesting and winter grounds.

Horse Island is about two miles from the harbour mouth and has an old lighthouse tower. On the face of it an easy enough swim ... apart from the very strong currents!

We were strong 15 year old lads who had swum in the sea here since we were aged 5, and who regularly swam to the Island many times, weather permitting during the summer months.

Anyway, on this particular swim the weather was perfect sea state, smooth with the odd ripple, simply nice. So off we headed for the island, through the harbour mouth, carefully dodging the jellyfish, whose sting could ruin our swim. We continued heading across, to pass the breakwater at 1 mile, then sharp turn to port, before having to push hard against the current, putting on our afterburners so to speak.

We landed on the only good sandy beach on Horse Island. We relaxed and had a look around the Island for a couple of hours, watching the tides throughout. A good time had by us both, typical 15 year olds messing about with time to spare.

Eventually it was time to swim back. So off we go, with the current still doing its worst. We take the required starboard turn at the end of the breakwater, enjoying our swimming to the harbour mouth. We just got as far as the middle of the mouth, heading for the harbour light and then all hell let loose. We didn't realise there was a blind spot and we couldn't hear the sound of the siren blasting from an approaching ship. From the surface of the water we neither heard nor saw anything.

Then, all of a sudden from the blind side of the harbour wall appears the MV Glen Sannox from Arran going at a fair rate of knots.

Her siren sounding, with her twin screw in full motion she was shifting through the water. Luckily she could also slow down pretty quickly too.

Well, you never saw two 15 year olds swim faster! We must have broken the Olympic record; our hearts were as the saying goes 'in our mouths', hearts pumping like crazy.

We swam into the small inner harbour which was next to the Glen Sannox berth. The passengers on deck watching us, was bad enough, but the skipper (Master) shouting through his megaphone, telling us how silly and stupid we were, though he used different terminology, was something else to be heard.

As we reached the sand in the berth, I look up at the bridge on the boat and in all the excitement had missed who it was who was shouting – only my grandad! He was indeed the skipper.

Needless to say, we received a good telling of from him, my dad, my uncles and all the sailors. If that wasn't bad enough our punishment was to be banned from swimming for a couple of weeks.

Subsequently, whenever I visited my grandad, the first thing he would always remind me of was that eventful day. He was a fine chap and even to this day I feel so ashamed that I put him through that worry.

This all happened back in July 1963 and in case you were wondering, yes, we did swim across to Horse Island again many, many times.

However, we always made sure we swam between the ferry times!

A Swim To Remember Tylor

Dave Stevens

On June 28th 2013 I held my son in my arms as he died. Something I never thought would happen.

I hugged him until his mum got to us. I watched in her face our world crumble. My son, Tylor, had passed away after suffering from a stroke that was not diagnosed and then not treated correctly.

The ensuing grief was a horrid thing that enveloped our life and is hard to fully describe here. When you lose a child everything changes. From the way you see yourself, to the way others see or react towards you. You lose all confidence in everything. Add to this, the stress of how Tylor was mistreated and the ongoing battle we had proving the lack of care received. This process took nearly a year, but I did it to hopefully stop the same happening to someone else. During that time our lives just stopped.

We would make sure our daughter, Leah, got to school, but I didn't work for nearly a year as money had no relevance now. I had to be with my family and we had to find a way through the troubled water. Being the devoted mum Samantha was, it was understandable that she fell apart. She never left the house at all for 6 months. We would shop for food in a different shop away from town and as I write 3 years on, Sam still has not set foot in our own town.

I had dealt with all the arrangements myself despite in the first 6 months never sleeping at night, such dark nights in my soul. I knew early on I still had a job to do and that job was to hold my family together. So, I set about in my mind thinking how I would rebuild our lives as best I could.

I pursued the Trust that was at fault and our complaints had been upheld fully. Little help to our family, but possibly to others. Gradually we started to rebuild our lives. It was difficult though as slowly it became as if Tylor had never been here. Over time, less people visited and less people spoke his name. This part was unbearable as we had lost our beautiful boy aged 17, just months away from his 18th birthday, which he had been busy planning. On the day we should have been celebrating we just had family and a few close friends round and we fell to bits. Witnessing the look in their eyes was so hard for me, such sadness at looking upon a broken family. I really did not want this to happen again on future birthdays.

At first, it was a day to day thing putting structure back into my life. I started to swim on Friday evenings at our local pool for an hour. I hadn't swum for many years, having focussed on earning and paying a mortgage. In my early childhood years I learned to swim in By Brook, a small stream near Box in Wiltshire. Also, I spent many hours of fun in the River Avon and playing in the fields of Lacock near Chippenham.

So I swam on a Friday evening. I would be constantly thinking, constantly trying. I was slowly rebuilding our lives, starting with me. I used swimming as a scaffold around my life once a week to build a structure that would hold me up almost like a crutch for my soul. It may sound deep and it was, constantly thinking my family was watching me needing to relearn even if they didn't know it. Tylor's 19th birthday came and went with no fuss, lots of tears and pain, but no fuss. I was becoming stronger.

We were a year in and I was now swimming twice a week and working again. I had decided I did not want Tylor's 20th birthday to be the pain of his 18th or the quietness of his 19th. How could you calibrate when he's not here, when he's been taken too soon from us? There was so much hurt so much pain, so many tears; my grief is but a tear that falls into the sea and when I find it I will stop.

I knew from early on I wanted to do something for the Make-A-Wish Foundation UK.

I had focused upon my swimming and wondered if I could use it like a tool to fix things? I was always good with my hands and as a plumber was always able to fix things but I couldn't fix losing Tylor. During one of the many dark nights I watched a short film on You Tube about a guy called Kev Brady swimming Lake Windermere and a small light lit at the end of that long tunnel.

It was now January 2015 and I started to swim more. I had contacted Kev who by chance was a co founder of the charity Superhero Foundation, who inspire people to do things for themselves to help their children. In February I came down with bronchitis which stopped me swimming for two months. I was gutted as I knew I would miss out on my training. I had intended to swim Windermere on the anniversary of his passing in the June, I couldn't do this now. I was no athlete coming into this weighing in at nearly 22 stone. Once better I continued to swim. I thought I could swim the distance of Windermere in my local pool and get sponsored for Make-A-Wish, a little daft being 42 years old and it's the sort of thing you did when at school. My local pool agreed to give me a lane for the day on Tylor's 20th birthday. I was going to celebrate in style. In preparation, I trained 2-3 times a week and did some big 3-4 hour swims. I was not going to let this birthday be a repeat of his 18th or 19th.

On the day I was up early. I picked up my friend Jim who was going to marshal; well, sit at a table poolside with banners. At 6:30 am I got in the pool, I could only swim breaststroke at this point so that's what I did for 9 and a half hours. As I swam I noticed throughout the day friends and family popping in to give me a wave. I didn't see looks of pity on these faces but smiles instead. As hard as I know it was for Samantha to be in public I knew that was good for her. She could talk of him without people wanting to change the conversation; it was our son's birthday, something to celebrate. I'd started a Just Giving page for my swim and we had raised around £2,800 for Make-A-Wish. We created a happy day and the money would be like a birthday present to Tylor to give to other children to create special wishes making more smiles. There was no stopping me now and in the wake of a great day I had decided in my mind I would now attempt to actually swim Lake Windermere! Should I? Could I?

Shortly after I had completed my swim, Kev Brady was setting about his next challenge. He was attempting to swim the length of the River Severn and I had arranged to meet up at some point. I decided to start my open water training by swimming with him in the Severn. The first day I went to swim, Kev was having a day off as he was behind with his blog. "Damn!" I thought, but we met up and had a great chat. I sponsored him through my company, giving him two cheques, one signed and one not. I said I would sign that one on his back at Severn beach when he gets out. I bet he thought I was nuts but it was just a little fun and now I had to go to see him finish. The next time I went to swim with him he'd fallen ill, so that open water swim was not meant to be. I was now teaching myself to swim crawl. I had been following Kev's blogs and felt part of it all. So I went to see him at his finish and signed that cheque, sure enough, on his back. It was like rocket fuel for me and my swimming. In all of this I could feel the positive effects it was having on me and hopefully my family would feed off this. I now needed to find some open water to train in and came across Lake 32 Waterland Outdoor Pursuits in the Cotswolds. It was November 2015 and my open water training would begin.

Kev convinced me to start a blog talking about my training. Me? Really? Would anyone be interested? So the very first morning, up early scraping frost off the van windshield, thinking I may die this morning and videoing myself, it came across how big the size of my challenge was to be. However, fuelled by the successes of Tylor's swim and Kev's in the Severn, 'A Swim To Remember' was born. I trained twice a week all through the winter in temperatures down to 2.1 degrees. I bought a 6XL cheap surfing wetsuit and remember all too well after getting back and having a hot shower, I was straight on eBay buying gloves and boots on express delivery ready for the following week.

That first day I arrived at 32 I felt as if it was always meant to be. I felt at home, at the time I didn't realise but the lake was sectioned off to a beach at one end where we had taken Tylor as a small boy. I dug out an old happy photo with the island I was now swimming around in the background.

It was always meant to be. Well, that's how it felt. I had never done anything like this before and I was going to put my all into it; for Tylor, for my family, for Make-A-Wish, for all those children we could help.

Of course my fitness would gain too. Early every Friday morning I was at the gate of that lake before most others. I parked up, took a few photos for my blog or would do a quick film and post it out. A lot of people got accustomed to my weekly blogs. I tried to make this as fun for everyone as I could and I hope it comes across that way. Yes it was serious, although I was going to make this journey fun so everyone enjoyed it too.

Things seemed to be slotting into place and one early swim at the lake I met Jason Aspinall, who again by chance, was swimming Windermere too. As we chatted, it transpired that he was booked to swim it the same day as me. Well, my day had been set in stone 21 years prior; fate was starting to play a hand. We became friends and although Jason was a much faster swimmer than me we became swim partners. We would banter, push each other on distances and check when swimming next. Swimming in the same water as him was now a common thing; something which on the day of Windermere would put my mind at ease.

I worked hard at fundraising and organised a plan. I would train right through winter, get some coaching, attend a few mini events to make it fun and help the blog not just be about me swimming. I was going to swim Weymouth bay in June, local Bowood Lake in July and a marathon 10km in August all as part of my training. What I didn't realise was how friendly open water swimmers are. From the first morning when a small chap, neoprene clad, asked if I was swimming then smiled when I said yes and jumped in, I have met so many lovely people, too many to name. I spent a day swimming 13km with Chris who was training to swim the Thames and when offered a place on the boat for my swim he jumped at the chance to return the favour. I'm so glad he did, again fate was at work.

 South West Swim - Swim Smooth Certified Coaching @SouthWestSwim

I was now very focused on the job in hand and had asked Jason Tait from South West Swim about coaching, knowing it would be good to have some help along the way. He had decided to sponsor a charity swimmer this year and after putting my reasons for what I was doing in we won it – wow! Now I had a coach this was getting serious and very helpful. I had my training, my training partner and a coach, we might even do this. We even had a bit of fundraising continuing as I'd kept my Just Giving page active which had now reached about £2,800.

I went up to Windermere in May to make arrangements and of course have a swim. I swam out into the middle of Windermere at 5:30 am on my own swimming into the mist, it was so tranquil. Tylor had put me there. I have always loved my son with a passion that every loving father knows but he had done this for me and he wasn't even here. It was breathtaking and I screamed at the top of my voice that day. I actually felt hurt and pain leave me in the middle of that lake. It was very moving.

I had been worrying about everything. Illness, injury, logistics, people, accommodation, you name it. Would my blog connect with people? Would they want to be part of this rollercoaster ride that I was using to rebuild our lives? Me talking about my son openly to hear his name, to see his photo on posters around the town, it had all come together ... and here I was, 7th September, sat in the boathouse at Langdale Chase, on the banks of Windermere at 4 am, wide awake! The boat we had picked up the night before had been charging on the jetty, it was still dark. I was going to swim with Tylor's pendant under my wetsuit. The donations had been coming in and it was working, people had connected to our journey. Jim, Marcus and Chris were in the boat and we would have points along the way where we would see our guests, about 16 of them who had come up. I did some stretching, something I don't usually do, ate some food and drank two pints of water (not easy at 4:30 am). I went down to the jetty where I filmed and wished Tylor a happy birthday. The lads were here, the boat ready and with a kiss from Sam, we were soon on our way.

I asked Chris to upload my birthday message to Tylor, first, then to start blogging live along the way. I felt really good and drew comfort from knowing Jason, my swim partner, was swimming from the opposite end and we would meet up somewhere in the middle for a 'Cotswold Open Water Swimmers high-five'.

The conditions were great, like glass at one point. I met up with guests and, of course Samantha and Leah, along the way, grabbing kisses from Sam which they videoed live.

There was a point in my swim, just before I met Jason coming up behind Bella Island, which was the best part.

The sun rose on my back, I could see the rays penetrating the water and a memory came flooding back of Tylor and Leah laughing while I swam with them on my back in the sea on a holiday in Wales many years earlier when they were small.

I truly felt like I was flying.

The moment I met Jason as planned was truly ace, then we swam on in our respective directions.

Chris jumped in to swim with me after our next meet up with family and off we went down the hard, long section of the lake. Despite the stretches I had done that morning my wrist was now playing up. I had made good time to the first 6 miles as we passed by Stalls Halt and with Chris by my side we swam on. As it got harder and my wrist hurt more, I recalled my coach saying, "Put your head down and just swim!" Also, I remember Jennie commenting, "JKS", which up until then I hadn't realised stood for 'Just Keep Swimming'.

I thought of Tylor fighting though surgeries, with me carrying him into surgery seven times not knowing if my boy would come back to me each time and the feeling of relief when he opened his eyes. I felt the love that was Samantha and Leah waiting for me at the end and with every painful stroke I swam on past each point, which opened up to another mile, then another. I took as long to swim the last 3 miles as I had taken to swim the first 7 miles! Inspired by knowing how many people had donated, there was no way I would get out of the water and into the boat.

As I continued swimming, two Hercules airplanes flew low overhead, which was a very fitting tribute, since they are our local planes with us living close to MoD Lyneham. When Tylor was small, we would park up at the end of the runway and watch them take off and land.

It was all perfect, even with the pain. As, in life, nothing is easy and good things need to be worked at.

Seeing Sam at the end and hugging her, I realised we had done it! We had created new happy memories with Tylor, something I never thought possible.

As I write this, we have so far raised over £8,500 which I know will help the 'Make-A-Wish' Foundation create smiles and happy memories for many families. Happy memories and smiles are a poor man's gold, so I feel I am a very wealthy man.

This truly was 'A Swim To Remember' – please see my blog: www.make-a-wish.org.uk/blog/a-swim-to-remember-tylor

When buying my Happy Wild Swimming cap the choice of colour was easy for me.

It had to be orange, as it is a very special colour to my family - Tylor's favourite colour - so no other colour will do!

Flipping Brilliant Swimming

Shaun Hales

This was my third season and the challenge had been to swim the Cabrera Crossing. Cabrera is an uninhabited islet in the Balearic Islands, located in the Mediterranean Sea off the southern coast of Majorca. Training proved too much, too soon and I eventually conceded to ill health.

My hope was soon rekindled in the form of an offer to join an English Channel relay team. It was never something I'd considered as I always thought it best to do a Channel swim as a solo. However, having met Jason, Rob and exuberant Jane I was committed to making it happen.

'Flipping Brilliant' was the team name and now we had to live up to it.

Two months of travelling to Dover and a punishing 6-7 days a week training plan later, we were bound as a team by mutual suffering.

So the budget vessel of our choice left Folkestone during the early hours of 'I'd rather be asleep o'clock' and wibbled along the coast to Samphire Hoe.

Jason started the swim and before you could say vomit I was leaping over the side to take over.

The whole day is a bit blurry but this swim will stay with me forever.

Swimming past a glowing Dover harbour, in clear deep water, with only the moonlight illuminating the bubbles flowing off my hands, I can honestly say it was one of the best times of my life.

By the time it was my turn to do my 4th swim section, my body was 78% jelly from the 12 hours of seasickness, which in turn had stopped me eating and drinking. I could see the cape on the French mainland but we weren't moving closer, Jason came up to me and broke the news I had to go in again, body now 99% jelly. I got up and lobbed myself over the side before I had a chance to barf.

Over the next hour they nearly pulled me out, disorientated and dehydrated I was swimming all over the place. Hallucinating and nearly hitting the prop I was glad when Jane finally took over to bring it home in 14 hours 23 minutes on Sangatte beach.

We were baptised in salt that day and will always remember it.

I learnt a few important things too ...

don't bother with ginger tea, don't take your Nan and never ever stop!

RECOMMENDED SUPPLIERS

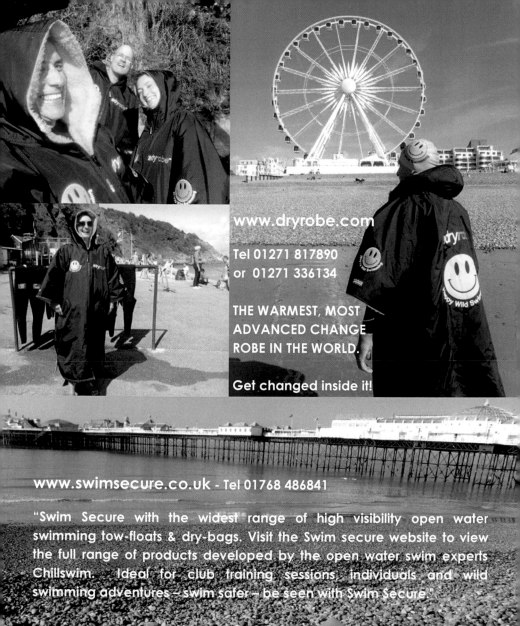

www.dryrobe.com

Tel 01271 817890
or 01271 336134

THE WARMEST, MOST ADVANCED CHANGE ROBE IN THE WORLD.

Get changed inside it!

www.swimsecure.co.uk - Tel 01768 486841

"Swim Secure with the widest range of high visibility open water swimming tow-floats & dry-bags. Visit the Swim secure website to view the full range of products developed by the open water swim experts Chillswim.   Ideal for club training sessions, individuals and wild swimming adventures – swim safer – be seen with Swim Secure."

SWIM SECURE

Acknowledgements

We would like to express our gratitude to the many swimmers both locally and around the World who continue to support the **Facebook Group: Happy Wild Swimming**

It was never envisaged that so many people would enjoy our simple pleasure of wearing a 'happy cap' while having fun swimming outside, in all weathers, at various locations around the World, often throughout the year.

A huge THANK YOU to each and every one of you!

The contributors - To those members who took the time to contribute their stories and photographs, memories, a slice of their lives, however brief or detailed it was, a special thank you. Without you caring enough to be supportive of this book it would not exist. We hope you are equally as happy seeing your words in print and proudly share them with your friends and family, maybe even with strangers.

Front cover artwork by Lynn Howarth - Our appreciation for kindly making the time to understand the concept of the 'happy cap' and combining it with her unique artistic flair to create the wonderful front cover image. The book contains stories which are reflections on swimmers' lives. The 'happy cap' reflection in the water provides a lovely affinity creating a stunning piece of artwork. Email: info@lynnhowarth.co.uk

Our cap supplier - Thanks to Richard and team for all your efforts and patience. The creation and subsequent productions have sometimes been a challenge for us all, not helped by our designs being awkward for the manual production necessary to achieve the product we required. You got us there and continue to provide the great quality swimming caps which allow the swimmers to show they are having happy times. You helped make our idea a reality and continue to keep the 'happy caps' coming.

Sophie Pierce: Beyond The Beach - Our personal thanks for opening our eyes in the early days to some local swims we have enjoyed exploring and for advice received.

Swimming products suppliers - Thanks to the genuinely Recommended Suppliers of the swimming items we regularly use, along with interim suppliers of additional items, as without them we would each have a less enjoyable time in and out of the water - swimmers would have far fewer smiles in their wardrobes and kit bags!

www.swimmingwithsmiles.com

Happy Swimming! – Happy Wild Swimming! – Happy Cold Swimming!

Happy Caps and other products available from: **www.altern8ives.com**

Index

Summer 2014